30-SECOND
RELIGION

30-SECOND
RELIGION

THE 50 MOST THOUGHT-PROVOKING RELIGIOUS BELIEFS,
EACH EXPLAINED IN HALF A MINUTE

Editor
Russell Re Manning

Contributors
Richard Bartholomew
Mathew Guest
Graham Harvey
Russell Re Manning
Alexander Studholme

Illustrations
Ivan Hissey

IVY PRESS

This edition published in the UK in 2018 by
Ivy Press
An imprint of The Quarto Group
The Old Brewery, 6 Blundell Street
London N7 9BH, United Kingdom
T (0)20 7700 6700 **F** (0)20 7700 8066
www.QuartoKnows.com

First published in hardback in 2015

© 2017 Quarto Publishing plc

British Library Cataloguing-in-
Publication Data
A CIP catalogue record for this
book is available from the
British Library

ISBN: 978-1-78240-591-7

This book was conceived,
designed and produced by
Ivy Press
58 West Street, Brighton BN1 2RA, UK

Creative Director **Peter Bridgewater**
Publisher **Jason Hook**
Editorial Director **Caroline Earle**
Art Director **Michael Whitehead**
Designer **Ginny Zeal**
Concept Design **Linda Becker**
Illustrator **Ivan Hissey**
Profiles & Glossaries Text **Nic Compton**
Assistant Editor **Jamie Pumfrey**

Printed in Hong Kong

10 9 8 7 6 5 4 3 2

CONTENTS

INTRODUCTION
Russell Re Manning

Religion is back. Of course, for millions of believers around the world it never really went away. Notwithstanding the confident predictions of 20th-century advocates of secularization, nor indeed the more aggressive declarations of the so-called "new atheists" of the 21st century, religious beliefs and practices continue to thrive. And no wonder—they are so fascinating, diverse, and intriguing.

This book is not about "religion"—surely no convincing single unified definition could ever suffice—but about religions. More precisely, it is about 50 prominent religions that between them span the spiritual life of the world—from ancient traditions with origins that have been lost in the mists of time and mythology to brand new religious movements.

Perhaps the most striking thing about religions is the dramatic variety of the beliefs and practices of the faithful. Religions are not monolithic institutions, but living communities of believers. While this makes them fascinating to study, the variety of religious beliefs and spiritual practices can make them a daunting prospect for the interested "lay person." Religious beliefs and practices can seem confusing to the uninitiated, the language used can be specialized and obscure, and the finer points of doctrinal debate can seem frankly about as relevant as the apocryphal medieval question about the number of angels able to dance on a pinhead. Fortunately, this book can help. In the pages that follow, the 50 key religions are summed up in plain English—no jargon and no waffle. The central beliefs and distinctive features of each religion are set out

Rich variety

Religion has been a part of everyday life for many cultures since antiquity. From major religions to less widespread sects, this book explores the diversity and symbolism of the world's religions.

accessibly and engagingly in less than the time it takes to offer a prayer. Each 30-second religion is presented alongside a single-sentence 3-second sermon for those in the spiritual fast lane, while for those taking the contemplative path, the 3-minute theology delves that bit deeper into the mysteries of the faiths.

The religions are organized into seven chapters. The first, **Indigenous Religions**, includes some of the oldest religions in the world, mostly closely related to particular cultures. In the second, **Eastern Spiritualities**, the major religious traditions of Asia are surveyed, while the third, **Abrahamic Traditions**, covers those traditions historically anchored in the Middle East that share a common lineage to Abraham. The next two chapters deal with the varieties of the world's most widespread religion: **European Christianities** treats those Christian denominations with historical roots in Europe, while **World Christianities** includes Christian churches with origins outside Europe. **Fusion Religions** focuses on those religions that combine elements from different traditions to create religious fusions and the final group, **New Religions**, introduces some of the major new religious movements of the 20th century. Along the way, we stop off at the seven key sacred texts, taking a look at some of the most profound and influential books of all time.

This book can be read it two ways. If you read it cover to cover—from Genesis to Revelation—you will get an excellent overview of the dazzling diversity of religions and the rich variety of their beliefs and practices. Otherwise, dip into individual entries here and there; you'll be surprised at some of the connections between religions. Go on, seek enlightenment!

Sacred texts

Throughout the centuries, the key tenets of many religious traditions have been passed down through sacred texts—many of which remain in use to this day.

神道

INDIGENOUS TRADITIONS

cosmos The universe, but particularly from the ancient Greeks' perspective of the universe as a harmonious whole—from the Greek word *cosmos*, meaning "order." The ancient Greeks saw the universe as completely interconnected and achieving a natural balance, similar to the view proposed today by the Gaia environmental movement.

devotee An enthusiastic, and possibly fanatic, follower of a religion. Not all followers of a religion are necessarily "devotees," which comes from the Latin word *devotus*, or "faithful." A more neutral term is "follower" or "adherent."

deity A god or other holy or sacred being. Most deities are the spiritual manifestation of a particular characteristic or life force, such as Ganesha, patron of science and learning in Hinduism, and Apollo, god of music in ancient Greece.

diaspora The spread of a people or culture from their ancestral home. Thus the diaspora of a religion is the multiple manifestations of that faith in various geographical locations. Spelled with a capital "D," it is usually interpreted as referring specifically to the migration of Jews from Israel. From the Greek *diaspeirein*, "to scatter seed."

divination A method of foretelling the future either by reading specially designed artifacts, such as tarot cards and rune stones, or interpreting omens in everyday life. Other forms of divination include: astrology, palmistry, crystal gazing, Chinese throwing sticks, and inspecting the entrails of a slaughtered animal. Most modern established religions, such as Christianity and Islam, condemn the practice.

indigenous Belonging to the locality where it is found; not imported from elsewhere. Most indigenous religions have developed over millennia and are closely entwined with the region's ecology.

medium A person who is said to contact the spirits of the dead and other paranormal forces and to act as an intermediary with the living. Contact is usually made when the medium falls into a trance and allows the spirit to use his or her body to communicate either verbally or through writing or other signs. The practice is prevalent in certain religions, such as Spiritualism and Voodooism.

metaphysical Relating to metaphysics, that is the study of the essential nature of being, including fundamental scientific truths and the spiritual dimension. The word is derived from the Greek words *metá* (meaning "beyond" or "after") and *physiká* (meaning "physical"). The main areas of modern metaphysics are: ontology (the nature of being), natural theology (the existence of God), and universal science (essential scientific principles).

monotheism The belief that there is only one God, as opposed to polytheism (many gods) and pantheism (God within nature). Judaism, Christianity, and Islam are prominent monotheistic faiths. From the Greek words *mono* ("single" or "alone") and *theos* ("God").

peyote A rounded, green cactus from Mexico from which the hallucinogenic alkaloid mescaline can be extracted. Use of peyote, also known as mescal button, is said to induce psychedelic trances and other out-of-body experiences. The plant has been used in religious rites and for medicinal purposes by Mexican tribes for over 3,000 years. Today, the Native American Church practices Peyotism.

polytheism The belief in more than one God. Most polytheistic faiths worship a number of deities, each of which represents different aspects of nature or the human character. These are used to explain the creation of the world and other natural phenomena. Most modern religions are polytheistic, including Hinduism, Confucianism, Taoism, and most African religions.

shaman A holy man or woman who acts as a medium or conduit between the physical world and the spiritual world. Shamans claim to channel supernatural forces to cure ailments and even control the weather. Although the term originates from Siberia, they are prevalent in most tribal cultures, especially Native American tribes.

talisman A piece of jewelry or other small object that is thought to possess magical properties and endow its wearer with special powers or to protect them from harm. The configuration of the stars when a talisman is created is sometimes said to invest it with a magical charge.

YORUBA
the 30-second religion

Yoruba traditional religion has

many similarities with other African traditional religions, including the ways in which it has creatively fused with other religions in the global Yoruba diaspora. People honor and seek the aid of one or more of the *orishas* (deities) and ancestors (those who have died but remain interested in their descendents) to support attempts to live fulfilled, healthy, and respectful lives. Many Yoruba believe in a "high God," Olodumare, above the many *orishas*, perhaps manifest *as* the many *orishas*. For them, Olodumare is the creator who started everything, but generally leaves the running of the earth to the *orishas*, each of whom is linked with specific phenomena. Shango, for example, is associated with lightning and electricity. In this fusion of animism and polytheism, deities exist in a rich web of relationships in a thoroughly social universe. A creative energy called "ashe" flows through everything. Public and private rituals, including sacrifices, are conducted to celebrate and enhance these relationships, which are expected to benefit the devotees as well as the deities or ancestors, especially by the sharing of "ashe." Religious knowledge is conveyed through divination systems, empowering stories, traditional practices, and dramatic festivals often involving masks and drums.

3-SECOND SERMON
Yoruba traditional religion is a vibrant way of seeking inspiration and energy from deities, ancestors, and other beings so that people can live fulfilled lives.

3-MINUTE THEOLOGY
The belief in a "high God," Olodumare, almost certainly originates from contact with Christians and Muslims. However, it should not be dismissed as a foreign import but celebrated as evidence of the vitality of a religion strong enough to also re-enchant modern processes, such as electricity generation and car making. In diaspora, Yoruba religious creativity is evident in Caribbean religions such as Santería, which fuses tradition with Roman Catholic Christianity, so that the *orishas* share costumes and feast days with "saints."

RELATED RELIGIONS
See also
ANIMISM
Page 18
ABRAHAMIC TRADITIONS
Pages 56–77
EUROPEAN CHRISTIANITIES
Pages 78–97

30-SECOND TEXT
Graham Harvey

Drawing on the traditional past while embracing the present, Yoruba celebrates health, respect, and fulfillment.

ABORIGINAL DREAMING

the 30-second religion

For Australian Aborigines, the Dreaming is the foundation of Law (rules) and Lore (teachings, often in the form of story, dance, or art) for living—it shapes how things are and should be. The Dreaming is also a fundamental aspect of creation. Before life, there was a dark, flat, featureless land. Beneath it existed (and will always exist) all possibilities. Occasionally, elements erupted through the surface, creating hills, valleys, rivers, and springs, even bringing forth sunlight. The elements were the ancestral forms of humans, kangaroos, bees, dingoes, and all life. As they traveled over the land, they created areas known as "countries." An ancestral caterpillar drops food, for example, and creates scrubland. Two dingoes fight, leaving pieces of flesh to become rocks. The ancestral forms interacted together: dancing, painting, sharing, and marrying. The ancestors then returned beneath the newly formed land surface, and their descendants (ordinary humans, kangaroos, bees, and dingoes) began to inhabit the land, following the lifestyles and rules established for them by their ancestral forms—the most important ones are those that require all inhabitants of countries to bear mutual responsibility for the well-being of that living community.

3-SECOND SERMON
The Dreaming is the continual formation of all life—together with rules for living—out of a preexisting chaos of fertile potential.

3-MINUTE THEOLOGY
The Dreaming is often presented as a collection of "just-so" stories about "creation-time." It is, in fact, a complex summary of the rights and responsibilities people have for dwelling cooperatively, without overconsumption, in specific regions. Its expression in art (from traditional rock art and body adornment to contemporary acrylics) and music (from funerary didgeridoo playing to urban fusions) now has global recognition. The Dreaming bears influence in legal land-rights cases as well as religious initiation rituals.

30-SECOND TEXT
Graham Harvey

The Dreaming is a potent mix of creation myth and ancestral lore dating back thousands of years, and has at its heart a message of responsibility.

ANIMISM

the 30-second religion

Animism is not in itself a religion, but as a belief system, is present in a number of religions. It refers to the worldviews of many indigenous people and some Pagans. In Animism, "persons" does not mean human or humanlike, but members of a multispecies community, perhaps including "rock persons" and "hedgehog persons." Adherents of animist religions claim to know that at least some rocks, animals, or plants are persons because they give and receive gifts, engage in conversations, or seem to act toward others intentionally. Humans, too, are only "persons" because they act in these ways. To respect other persons does not necessarily mean liking them. It means acknowledging they also have rights and interests. Persons can be killed, but only when necessary and always compassionately. Animist religions often feature shamans: experts in resolving interspecies misunderstandings (such as when humans insult hunted animals), knowing the whereabouts of others (such as distant food species), or combating aggressors (such as disease persons). Their work often involves dramatic trance rituals. Generally, animism is expressed in simple gift-giving to other persons, as when Native Americans offer tobacco or sage to elders or sacred beings.

3-SECOND SERMON
Animism is a way of seeing the world—including animate and inanimate objects—as a community of living "persons," all of which deserve respect.

3-MINUTE THEOLOGY
Animist beliefs play a key role in evolutionary explanations of religion. Some cognitive and evolutionary psychologists theorize that a belief in, for example, thunder and lightning being a manifestation of an angry spirit is "minimally counterintuitive," in that it fulfills intuitive assumptions while violating some of those assumptions in a small way. Such beliefs are attention grabbing and memorable and, thus, provide the basis for most religious convictions, as well as potentially being useful evolutionary adaptions.

RELATED RELIGIONS
See also
YORUBA
Page 14
MESOAMERICAN RELIGION
Page 22
SHINTO
Page 54

3-SECOND BIOGRAPHIES
DANIEL QUINN
1935–

DAVID ABRAM
1957–

30-SECOND TEXT
Graham Harvey

It's not just humans who have feelings, animals, plants, and rocks do, too—they all deserve respect.

NATIVE AMERICAN CHURCH

the 30-second religion

Religious consumption of peyote

cactus bulbs originated in remote antiquity among indigenous peoples in what is now Mexico. It spread northward rapidly from the 1880s, becoming a vital spiritual source in many reservation communities. Significant quantities (chewed or prepared in a tea) induce powerful visions, inspiring the founders and leaders ("roadmen") of the Native American Church (NAC), but milder brews heighten people's awareness and enable them to focus on concerns beyond their everyday troubles. Peyote is consumed sacramentally, not recreationally, because it is understood to come from the Creator's heart to bring healing, knowledge, and the motivation people need to lead healthy and moral lives. The NAC is the largest peyotist movement. Legally incorporated in the United States in 1918, it arose from the teachings of prophets, such as John Wilson and John Rave, who experienced peyote as a healer and guide, and who encouraged a fusion of indigenous and Christian practices. Jesus and the Bible, for example, are important to many NAC members. Indigenous traditional protocols blend local and continent-wide practices to make variations in NAC rituals and address specific communities' needs. The NAC encourages respect for the earth and the use of "natural" products.

3-SECOND SERMON
The Native American Church (NAC) is a pan-Native American religion that is best known for the use of peyote as a sacrament.

3-MINUTE THEOLOGY
The Native American Church or "Peyote Road" encourages sobriety, family care, self-reliance, and the unity of Native peoples. In addition to nightlong vigils that inspire unity, the NAC is respected for the antialcohol effects of peyote consumption and of its teaching. Legal struggles against the criminalization of peyote as a "drug" have led to freedom of religion laws that permit its sacramental use, including among Native Americans in U.S. prisons. NAC often works alongside indigenous traditionalists.

3-SECOND BIOGRAPHIES
QUANAH PARKER
1852–1911

JOHN RAVE
1856–1917

JOHN WILSON
1860–1901

JAMES MOONEY
1861–1921

30-SECOND TEXT
Graham Harvey

For NAC members, the hallucinogenic property of the peyote cactus is an essential source of profound spiritual inspiration.

MESOAMERICAN RELIGION

the 30-second religion

Prior to the Spanish conquest, a broad, common religious culture existed across Mesoamerica. Trade, similar language traits, and especially a reliance on corn agriculture by settled populations, with some large urban centers, unified the region. Over time and distance, significant diversity is also evident. Large, centralized empires (such as that of some Mayan groups) contrast with smaller societies, influencing spiritual diversity. From the civic rituals of urban centers to the shamanic healing rituals of villages, people sought to maintain harmony, such as by offering blood to enable deities to control cosmic processes, recording astronomical observations to maintain auspicious timing, or expressing gratitude to corn for its sacrificial gift of life. Purification ceremonies aided respectful relationships with nonhuman persons of these animist and polytheistic communities. Should, for example, someone drop corn on the ground, rituals apologized for the unintended insult to this sacred plant person. Temple complexes and pottery illustrate the religiously expressive art of the region, because they are often adorned with divine and shamanic beings. Dramatic polarities, such as night and day, male and female, and conflict and harmony, for example, could result in tension but were important in the continuous regeneration of life promoted by religious activities.

3-SECOND SERMON
Mesoamerica (from central Mexico to northwest Costa Rica) is typified by similar religions in which humans participate with other beings to keep the cosmos working.

3-MINUTE THEOLOGY
After the Spanish invasion, a tension between a single culture and local differences remains clear in various forms of Latin American Christianity, which often include elements from pre-Columbian traditions. Regional festivals and dance ceremonies are evidence of fusions between Catholicism and Mayan or other cultures. Pre-Christian pilgrimages continue by including saints among those addressed in prayers—and those expected to reciprocate by enhancing the well-being of the devout.

RELATED RELIGIONS
See also
ANIMISM
Page 18

30-SECOND TEXT
Graham Harvey

A common thread running through Mesoamerican religion was a desire to keep the cosmos in balance—sometimes involving human bloodletting.

SHENISM

the 30-second religion

Shenism identifies the shifting

creative fusions of a distinctively Chinese-style spirituality. It shares many properties with traditional Chinese medicine, and popular religious activities often make use of dominant Buddhist, Confucian, and/or Taoist ideas, practices, officials, and locations. People visit shrines and temples, seek the ritual services of priests and monks, and make use of sacred texts and talismans. Whether or not people identify as members of the more organized forms of those religions can be contentious. The localized and kinship foundation of much of Chinese popular spirituality gives it a place among indigenous religions. This is particularly true when Shenism involves mediums to communicate with ancestors (named members of a family who, although dead, are still deemed to be interested in their descendants' well-being), and the use of divination. The word *shen* has a wide range of meanings, perhaps illustrated by the similar potential of one of its English translations, "spirit." Both words might refer to metaphysical entities (ancestors, ghosts, local deities, or beings who speak through mediums), or they might also refer to states of consciousness and refined internal energies, suggesting practices of focusing attention, meditation, trance, or seeking health and fulfillment.

RELATED RELIGIONS
See also
MAINSTREAM BUDDHISM
Page 36
TAOISM
Page 48
CONFUCIANISM
Page 50

30-SECOND TEXT
Graham Harvey

3-SECOND SERMON
Shenism is a recent label for the varieties of popular religious practices in China that draw on, but are not officially involved in, Buddhism, Confucianism, or Taoism.

3-MINUTE THEOLOGY
A tension between "worldly" interests (seeking personal and family health, wealth, and harmony) and "other-worldly" interests (pursuing beneficial reciprocal relationships with ancestors and deities, and well-being for ancestors and oneself in future states, such as in heaven or in rebirth) is crucial to the relationship between Shenism and more organized religions. There are few official practices and teachings concerning such matters, but popular or democratic desires, needs, and fears encourage the self-taught feel and diversity of Shenism.

Shenism—the worship of shens (deities or spirits)—is a collection of Chinese folk religions influenced by Buddhist, Confucian, and Taoist principles.

ZOROASTRIANISM

the 30-second religion

3-SECOND SERMON

Probably the oldest living religion, Zoroastrianism identifies the struggle between good and evil as the context of all existence.

3-MINUTE THEOLOGY

Zoroastrian philosophical influence on the theologies and cosmologies of monotheistic religions was foundational. Relatively small populations of Zoroastrians survive now, primarily in Iran and India. Variations in practice occur, such as in the timing of Nav Ruz, the new year festival, celebrated at spring equinox in Iran to symbolize the victory of light over darkness, but in August in India because Parsis there have not adjusted their calendars for leap years.

Around 3,000 years ago an Iranian prophet, now known as Zarathushtra (or Zoroaster following Greek pronunciation), is said by Zoroastrians (or Parsis in India) to have initiated the religion's emphasis on "good thoughts, good words, good deeds." A cosmic struggle between good and evil not only confronts humans as the context of all existence, but takes place in the everyday moral choices that each person has to make. Some Zoroastrians emphasize the moral struggle as the key teaching—the freedom of choice between good and evil. The struggle involves the eternal Wise Lord, Ahura Mazda, in opposition to a destructive adversary, Ahriman. A number of other beings, the Beneficial Immortals, are present in the constituent elements of the cosmos and in the struggle. Rather than pollute earth, water, or fire, Zoroastrians traditionally exposed their dead on high towers, where vultures consumed their flesh. By combating "bad thoughts, bad words, bad deeds," Zoroastrians work toward the purification and proper ordering of the cosmos. Rituals led by priests, individual action, and community life are guided by a variety of sacred texts—such as the *Gathas*, a series of hymns that encourage vigilance against all negative thoughts or acts.

RELATED RELIGIONS

See also
ABRAHAMIC TRADITIONS
Pages 56–77
EUROPEAN CHRISTIANITIES
Pages 78–97

3-SECOND BIOGRAPHIES

ZARATHUSHTRA (ZOROASTER)
fl.c.5000 BCE

DARIUS 1
c.558–486 BCE

30-SECOND TEXT

Graham Harvey

Ancient and mystical, Zoroastrianism is as much philosophy as it is religion—with the struggle between good and evil, order and chaos at its core.

EASTERN SPIRITUALITIES

EASTERN SPIRITUALITIES
GLOSSARY

asceticism The practice of punishing the body to achieve greater spiritual awareness.

atheist Someone who doesn't believe in the existence of God or a Higher Being.

Brahman The Hindu priestly caste. Literally, one who has control of *brahma*, the sacred word or spirit.

caste The groups into which Hindu society is divided. There are four main divisions: Brahmans (teachers and priests); Kshatriyas (soldiers and rulers); Vaishyas (farmers and merchants); and Shudras (servants and laborers). In addition there are many hundreds of subdivisions, relating to different trades and family lineages. Caste continues to inform the way in which Hindus get married, worship, and eat together.

dharma From the verb *dhr*, "to uphold," dharma is a natural law that sustains the universe. It is subtle and difficult to discern. In Hinduism, the term refers, above all, to the way in which human beings conform to this natural law: in custom, religious code, rites of passage, and caste duty. Each person has their own dharma, or *svadharma*, a natural way of being in the world. *Stridharma*, for instance, is the dharma of women. In Buddhism, dharma refers to the teaching of The Buddha.

enlightenment Translation of the Sanskrit word *bodhi*, meaning "awakening"—seeing, for the first time, the true nature of reality.

guru A spiritual leader or teacher. Literally, one who is "weighty."

kami A title given to spirits in the Shinto religion, referring to invisible forces of nature or personified spiritual beings.

karma Literally, "action." Karma is the impersonal force that propels us from one lifetime to the next and gives shape to the fate of our present lives. Originally, strongly connected to ritual action, The Buddha reinterpreted karma to mean the intention behind our actions, removing it from the control of priests. It is a law of the universe, so it is incorrect to talk of punishment and reward. Virtuous actions naturally produce pleasant circumstances, and nonvirtuous, unpleasant. It should not be understood as pure fatalism or determinism: bad karma can be purified and good karma freshly generated.

Mahayana Literally, the "great" (*maha-*) "vehicle" (*-yana*). A later, more spiritual version of the Buddhist vision.

mysticism A religious approach to life that stresses intuition and direct experience of the divine.

nirvana The end of the mainstream Buddhist path, the end of rebirth. The opposite of samsara, or "wandering" from one lifetime to the next. Nirvana literally means a "blowing out." It is not the extinction of the person, but the extinction of the three fires of greed, hatred, and delusion. The Buddha was silent about where he was going after death: nirvana is beyond words, beyond existence or nonexistence. Also used in Hinduism, where the term *moksha*, or "liberation," is more common.

quasi-theistic Sharing certain features of theism, the philosophy that the universe is created and controlled by God, or a Supreme Being.

rebirth/reincarnation The belief, common to most Eastern religions, that death is not the end, but is followed by another life. The spiritual goal, then, is to bring about the end of this wearisome process. See *karma* and *nirvana*.

renunciate Someone who has given up, or "renounced" ordinary worldly life to concentrate on spiritual affairs, living as a monk or nun in a monastery or hermitage, or perhaps as a wandering ascetic, who begs for alms.

tao Often translated as "the way." An elusive mystical law or principle of the universe that one should attune oneself to. Taoism is an enigmatic, mystical interpretation of this idea, while Confucianism is more worldly and practical. See *dharma*.

Vajrayana Tantric Buddhism. Literally, the "vehicle" (-*yana*) of the Vajra, a term that originally referred to a thunderbolt weapon of the Hindu gods, but which in Buddhism means the indestructible nature of the enlightened mind.

Vedas The earliest Hindu religious texts, describing the rituals and theology of the Brahman priests.

yoga Literally, "joining"—as in the joining of oneself to God or the spiritual dimension. Thus, there is the yoga of knowledge, the yoga of work, the yoga of devotion, and, more familiarly, the yoga of spiritual and physical exercises.

Zen A school of East Asian Buddhism. "Zen" is a Japanese term, from the Chinese *chan*, itself from the Sanskrit *dhyana*, meaning "meditation." Prolonged meditation cuts through the rational mind to reveal the experience of enlightenment.

HINDUISM

the 30-second religion

3-SECOND SERMON
God is one and beyond form. God appears in many different forms. God lives in the heart. God contains the entire universe. God is everywhere.

3-MINUTE THEOLOGY
Hinduism is polymorphic monotheism. The gods express different aspects of divine reality, a cosmic spirit that exists inside and outside the individual. Shiva embodies power, Vishnu righteousness, and Devi, the goddess, the sweet or ferocious energy of mother or lover. Each manifests itself in different forms, marries other deities, raises divine families, uniting different traditions and creating new matrices of devotion. A Hindu worships one or many gods, depending on family upbringing, community, or personal choice.

Hindus believe that we are all continually reincarnated, lifetime after lifetime. Our fate is determined by karma, the moral worth of our previous actions. The spiritual goal is to put an end to rebirth and be united with God. This is achieved through the path of knowledge (via study, yoga, meditation, and ascetic practice, one experiences the identity of one's own soul with the cosmic spirit) and the path of devotion (praising and worshipping God). Worldly activities—the pursuit of wealth, power, love, and pleasure—must be performed in harmony with dharma, the natural law of the universe. Dharma has divided society into castes, rigidly categorizing families in terms of power, purity, prestige, and occupation. The Brahmans are the priestly caste. Their scriptures, the Vedas, are some 4,000 years old and define orthodoxy. Hinduism is the meeting of this big tradition, with many local little traditions— adapting and absorbing. Mythically, this process is expressed as big gods manifesting as little gods, or marrying goddesses. Hinduism is, thus, a loose assemblage of communities and sects— of various practices and traditions—like a large, extended family.

RELATED RELIGIONS
See also
MAINSTREAM BUDDHISM
Page 36
MAHAYANA BUDDHISM
Page 40
JAINISM
Page 42
SIKHISM
Page 44

3-SECOND BIOGRAPHIES
SHANKARA
c.788–820

RAMANUJA
c.1017–1137

RAMAKRISHNA
1836–1886

MOHANDAS (MAHATMA) GANDHI
1869–1948

RAMANA MAHARSHI
1879–1950

30-SECOND TEXT
Alexander Studholme

Hindus believe in a universal God, who takes on many forms.

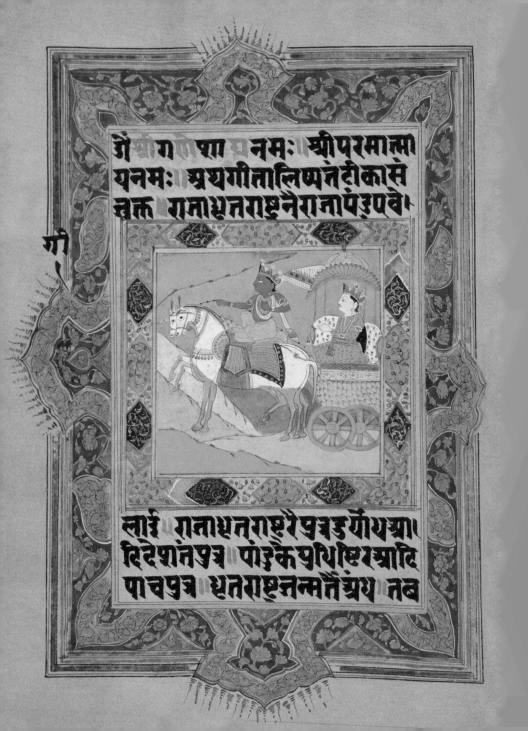

ॐ गणेशाय नमः श्रीपरमात्मा
यनमः अथगीताल्लिख्यतेटीकास
हित रानाधृतराष्ट्रनैराजापांडुपवे

लारे रानाधृतराष्ट्रैपुत्रइयोंधयात्रा
दिदेशंतत्र पांडुकेयुधिष्ठिरआदि
पाचपुत्र धृतराष्ट्रतन्मैंत्रयथ तब

BHAGAVAD GITA

The Bhagavad Gita (or "Song of the Lord") is quite possibly the most famous Hindu text of all. Its popularity lies in the fact that it is a concise synthesis of various Hindu ideas and, also, that it presents an approach to the spiritual path that is suitable for all, not just priests and hermits.

Dating from c.250 BCE, the Bhagavad Gita is part of the great Hindu epic, the Mahabharata, which tells of the cousinly rivalries of two branches of the same extended family. On the eve of a terrible battle between the clans, the Hindu God Krishna (the "lord" of the title), who appears initially in the guise of a charioteer, preaches this "song," or sermon, to a warrior called Arjuna. Arjuna is reluctant to fight and wants to escape to a life of meditation. He hopes he will then be free from the effects of negative actions, which keep human beings bound to the endless cycle of rebirth. Krishna responds by telling him that he must fight: it is his caste duty as a warrior. It is, moreover, impossible to avoid the effects of action: even hermits have physical bodies and must act in certain ways; and besides, many of them are hypocrites, apparently uninvolved with the world, but secretly seething with frustrated desires. The only actions that do not bind the individual to life in the world are sacrificial actions.

However, instead of ritual sacrifice, Krishna requires an internal sacrifice. He argues that the spiritual life can be lived in the world—even in the heat of battle—if actions are performed out of a sense of religious duty, with one's mind set not on any personal reward, but in an attitude of devotion to God. It is a matter of conforming one's actions to the will of God, who exists within the heart. Krishna then manifests an awe-inspiring cosmic form, which contains the universe. Whoever loves God, he explains, is loved by God. Devotees live in Krishna and Krishna lives in them.

Krishna and Arjuna prepare for battle—the Bhagavad Gita expounds the main tenets of the Hindu faith in poetic, inspirational language.

C.250 BCE
Bhagavad Gita written

c.800
Sankaracharya's commentary brings wider audience

1290
Jnaneshvara writes Marathi commentary

1785
First English translation

1823
Translated into Latin

1909
Swami Swarupananda's English translation

MAINSTREAM BUDDHISM

the 30-second religion

The Buddha was a renunciate
holy man who stepped outside the mainstream Indian religion of the Brahman priests. He dispensed with rituals and speculation about God, teaching an intensely pragmatic path of mental cultivation, whose goal was the end of suffering. Suffering, Buddha said, is the inevitable result of the way in which the individual instinctively shores up the ego by grasping at what is pleasant and reacting against what is unpleasant. Realistically, pain is unavoidable and, more subtly, because things are always changing, so, too, is the difficulty of experiencing pleasant states slipping away. By fully appreciating the impermanent flow of experience—and the fact that everyone dies—one develops a dispassionate attitude, which is ultimately rooted in the discovery that the ego is itself an insubstantial fiction and that who we really are is beyond all thoughts of the "I." In this life, nirvana, the goal, is literally the "blowing out" of these compulsive tendencies—the three fires of greed, hatred, and delusion—denoting the complete turning around of a person from neurotic egoism to a state of blissful peace and the selfless freedom to be naturally loving toward others. At death, nirvana is the end of all rebirth.

3-SECOND SERMON
The Buddha's first sermon taught four truths: suffering, the origin of suffering, the end of suffering (nirvana), and the path to the end of suffering.

3-MINUTE THEOLOGY
Buddhist meditation consists of two combined disciplines: concentration and insight. By concentrating on an object, such as the breath, the mind withdraws from sensory experience and thoughts, developing states of calm and joy. Insight is the inculcated "seeing" of the impermanent flow of phenomena, in which the ego cannot be found. This eradicates a mistaken view of reality, which is the underlying basis of neurotic, emotional tendencies.

RELATED RELIGIONS
See also
HINDUISM
Page 32
MAHAYANA BUDDHISM
Page 40
JAINISM
Page 42

3-SECOND BIOGRAPHIES
THE BUDDHA
c.563–483 BCE

BUDDHAGHOSA
5th century BCE

30-SECOND TEXT
Alexander Studholme

Buddhists do not believe in a personal God, but strive to end suffering and attain the ultimate goal of enlightenment—nirvana—by living a selfless life.

အာဂစ နာဒဘ္ဘာဝသ်ာဘဝါသိက္ိဒဿ
နာဂစီသ နဲ့"အဟံဟ်ိသေနာယာဂစ္စ
ဒနေဝတသ္ပကရေကာဓမ္ဗိကတိကတ္တ
ဝင်္ဂဟေတ္တာစိဝရကောလ်သမယံ အ
ဒဝေါ၊ကယသ်မာနီအာဝုသောစိဝ
ရေဝသုံ"အာယသ္မာဒာနန္ဒေ၁ဉ
က်ိရာဘိက္ခုဝေဘိက္ခအ္ဆ္ဌေကစိဝရ္ံပ
သာန်္"နေဒံဘိက္ခုဝေအလ္ပသန္ဌနိုဝါ၊ပ
ဘဓ်"ပစ္ဂဟေတ္တာယာဝစိဝရကောလ
ဘစိဝရံနာမသေနာယရဝါဂန္ကာမော
တံပဟ်ကေယျအာဂစနာဘာဒဘ္ဘာဝ
စ္ဌကစိဝရနို်"စိဝရကာလသမယော
ယဂိယံပါ စိတ်ိယ်"အတ္ထဝေကဒ်
လသမယံအ တ်ိက္ကာဓတ္တနိသဂိယ်
စ္ဂါန"အ ရေကစိဝ

PALI CANON

There are three versions of the Buddhist canon,

the earliest of which is the Pali Canon. The other two are the Chinese and Tibetan Canons, which contain the later teachings of Mahayana and Vajrayana (or Tantric) Buddhism. From the beginning of the first millennium, Indian Buddhist missionaries had traveled along the Silk Road into China. Then, at the end of the millennium, texts were taken across the Himalayas into Tibet to escape the Muslim invasions of India, which brought about the demise of Buddhism in the sub-continent.

All three canons are known as *tripitika*, or "three baskets": containing *vinaya* (monastic discipline), *sutra* (discourses), and *abhidharma* (scholastic treatises). The process of bringing together a definitive collection of teachings began at the First Buddhist Council, which was held shortly after the death of The Buddha in c.480 BCE, when 500 enlightened monks convened to recite everything from memory. A number of Buddhist sects subsequently developed in India, of which the Theravada ("teachings of the elders") became preeminent, spreading to Sri Lanka and Southeast Asia.

The Pali Canon is understood by Theravadins to be a version of the early canon brought to Sri Lanka in the 3rd Century BCE. Pali is the name of the language used: close to the one spoken by The Buddha and a simpler form of the elite Sanskrit language used by the Brahman priests. According to tradition, it would be another 150 years before the teachings were first written down, which must have come as some relief to those responsible for maintaining this feat of memory. The sutra basket alone contains 34 long discourses, 152 medium-length discourses, and many hundreds of shorter sermons. In order to authenticate themselves as the "word of The Buddha," the later canons argued that the Mahayana teachings were received in dreams and visions from The Buddha, who continued to exist in a spiritual form.

A page from the Pali Canon—in
the Burmese language.

563 BCE
The Buddha is born

483 BCE
Death of The Buddha;
First Buddhist Council

250 BCE
Creation of Pali Canon

29 BCE
Pali Canon transcribed
onto palm leaves

1868
Inscribed on 729 marble
slabs in Mandalay, Burma

1893
Incomplete version
printed in Siam
(modern-day Thailand)

1900
First complete edition
printed in Burma

1956
Sixth Buddhist Council
approves new version

MAHAYANA BUDDHISM

the 30-second religion

In Mahayana Buddhism, the historical Buddha is regarded as a physical manifestation of the true body of The Buddha—a formless, cosmic, spiritual body, which is also the ultimate nature of reality itself. Thus, the entire universe exists within The Buddha. This formless body also emanates many other intermediary, nonphysical divine forms: Buddhas and other enlightened beings that may be contacted through devotional practices. These divine forms are also the source of freshly revealed scriptures, sutras, which describe these devotional practices and, also, a new metaphysics. Again and again, reality is compared with a magical illusion or dream. All phenomena are "empty"—that is, they lack any discernible substantial essence and have no independent existence outside of the mind. The spiritual path no longer ends in nirvana—a state of peace that is the end of rebirth—but involves a continuous return to embodied existence, out of compassion for others, culminating in the achievement of complete Buddhahood. Progress on the path involves cultivating this compassion, alongside insight into "emptiness." More succinctly, all that is required is to purify the mind, allowing the inherent qualities of ultimate reality—the Buddha nature that exists within all beings—to shine through.

3-SECOND SERMON
Mahayana ("the great vehicle") is an amplified, more spiritualized Buddhist vision, adding devotionalism and a complex metaphysics to the psychological pragmatism of the original teachings.

3-MINUTE THEOLOGY
Mahayana Buddhism delights in paradox and shifting perspectives. Devotees aspire to be reborn in the realm of Amitabha, the Buddha of Endless Light, who actually exists within each person as the true nature of the mind. The path involves the laborious saving of countless suffering beings. But, upon investigation, all beings are "empty." There are, really, no beings and so ... no path. Everything is perfect as it is: there is nothing to do except relax.

RELATED RELIGIONS
See also
MAINSTREAM BUDDHISM
Page 36
TAOISM
Page 48

3-SECOND BIOGRAPHIES
NAGARJUNA
c.150–250 CE

BODHIDHARMA
c.5th/6th century

GURU PADMASAMBHAVA
c.8th century

NICHIREN
1222–1282

30-SECOND TEXT
Alexander Studholme

Buddha exists within all beings and is the true nature of reality—but what is reality?

JAINISM

the 30-second religion

Jainism—from *jina*, "conqueror"— emerged in India at the same time as Buddhism and presents an alternative version of the renunciate path. Its goal is the freeing of the soul from its coating of karma, leading to omniscience and, after death, the end of reincarnation and eternal life alongside other liberated souls, in a realm at the top of the universe. As in Buddhism, karma is the result of passion and action. However, in contrast to The Buddha's emphasis on meditation, the Mahavira—the "great hero," the founder of Jainism—prioritized the practice of strict self-restraint and severe austerities (particularly, fasting), in order to burn off karma. Jains also lay great stress on nonviolence and vegetarianism, because animals and even plants contain souls. Serious engagement with the path is, inevitably, the preserve of renunciate ascetics. Lay people support this endeavor, keep core vows as best they can, and prepare for renunciation in the future. Although there is no doctrine of a creator, Jains do worship God as the supreme spirit, which is the potential of all souls and immediately apparent in the Mahavira and other liberated teachers in his lineage, who, therefore, become the focus of devotion.

3-SECOND SERMON

Jainism is an ascetic and gentle religion, the source of the Hindu concept of *ahimsa*, "nonviolence," a cornerstone of the political philosophy of Mahatma Gandhi.

3-MINUTE THEOLOGY

Jains vow to abstain from killing, sexual activity, lying, stealing, and becoming attached to possessions. The first of these, compassionate nonviolence, is regarded as the supreme religious duty. Monks and nuns carry light brooms to brush aside any insects in their path and wear face masks to prevent the accidental inhalation of flies. Similarly, they drink only filtered water, are forbidden from lighting fires and digging the earth, and must generally move about with great care.

RELATED RELIGIONS

See also
HINDUISM
Page 32
MAINSTREAM BUDDHISM
Page 36

3-SECOND BIOGRAPHIES

MAHAVIRA
c.599–527/510 BCE

UMASVATI
c.2nd century BCE

30-SECOND TEXT

Alexander Studholme

All life is sacred and must not be harmed; to achieve omniscience karma must be shed through strict self-control and austerity.

SIKHISM

the 30-second religion

Sikhism is a Hindu sect that is
rooted in a lineage of ten gurus from the
Punjab, the north Indian territory where most
of the religion's adherents still live. Its two chief
characteristics are an ardent devotion to God
and an ethos of martial valor, both shaped by
the experience of living as a Hindu majority
under Muslim Mughal rule. The first guru, Guru
Nanak, was a wandering bard and mystic who
sang praises to a formless God that belongs
exclusively to neither Hindus nor Muslims, but
unites them both. The tenth guru, Guru Gobind
Singh, was a warrior poet who institutionalized
the duty to bear arms in the face of oppression.
Sikh worship involves the singing of hymns and
the recitation of the name of God, developing
love toward humanity and the divine, and
leading, eventually, to the end of reincarnation
in the experience of ultimate unity with God.
The Adi Granth, the holy book containing these
hymns, is the central focus of the Sikh place of
worship, or *gurdwara*, the most famous of
which is the Golden Temple in Amritsar. Sikhs
do not become renunciates, have no idols,
eschew caste restrictions, and value honest
labor and social service.

3-SECOND SERMON
Sikhs worship God,
who exists beyond all
appearances and who is
universally available to
all, whether they be
Hindu, Muslim, or of
any other creed.

3-MINUTE THEOLOGY
The Sikh turban is a badge
of identity that derives
from the first of five
precepts, or "k"s. The
Sikh male is traditionally
required never to cut his
hair (*kes*) as a sign of
spiritual strength. He is
also meant to wear or carry
a comb (*kangha*), an iron
bracelet (*kara*), a short
undergarment (*kacch*), and
a sword or dagger (*kirpan*),
which symbolize orderly
spirituality, protection and
unity with God, restraint,
and a readiness to fight.

RELATED RELIGIONS
See also
HINDUISM
Page 32

3-SECOND BIOGRAPHIES
GURU NANAK
1469–1539

GURU GOBIND SINGH
1666–1708

30-SECOND TEXT
Alexander Studholme

*"Realization of Truth
is higher than all
else. Higher still is
truthful living."*
Guru Nanak

GURU GRANTH SAHIB

Adherents of most religions believe their holy

books are more than just books. Which is why it's not surprising to
see Sikhs bow before their holy book, the Guru Granth Sahib. Nor is it
surprising that they believe you should cover your head and take your
shoes off in its presence, or that it's rude to turn your back on it. As
for putting a religious text to bed every night and uncovering it every
morning—superficially that might seem to be taking things too far. That is
until you realize that for Sikhs the Guru Granth Sahib is not just a book—
it's the manifestation of an actual guru. So, how did this 1,420-page tome
go from being a book called Adi Granth to a guru called Granth Sahib?

It all started with the first guru, Nanak, who discovered that turning
his teaching into rhymes and setting them to a tune was an effective
way of remembering them. He composed 974 such hymns (or *shabads*).
As the Sikh religion spread, an authoritative source of teaching was
required, and so the second guru, Angad, wrote Nanak's verses down,
adding 62 of his own. It is said that the Gurmukhi alphabet was invented
for the purpose. Inevitably, however, inaccurate copies began to emerge
and so, in 1604, the fifth guru, Arjan, created a definitive version,
approved by the last of the original Sikh disciples. It included another
2,218 hymns written by Arjan and 1,586 by his two immediate
predecessors, and was called Adi Granth, or the "first scripture."

The 6th, 7th, and 8th gurus were not composers, but the 9th guru Tegh
Bahadar and his son Gobind Singh resumed the project. Before he died,
however, Gobind proclaimed there would be no more human gurus.
Instead, he collated a new version of the Adi Granth, including 116 hymns
written by his father, and conferred upon it the title "Guru of the Sikhs,"
whereupon it was renamed Guru Granth—the "sahib" was added as a
mark of respect. Gobind Singh's own compositions were themselves
published and venerated by Sikhs as the Dasam Granth.

1469
Guru Nanak is born

1604
Adi Granth published

1698
Dasam Granth
published

1706
Guru Granth Sahib
published

1708
Guru Gobind dies

1864
First printed copy of
Guru Granth Sahib

1960
First English translation

**A Sikh scholar works on a handwritten
version of the Guru Granth Sahib.**

TAOISM

the 30-second religion

3-SECOND SERMON
Taoism is a mystical way
of life, a cornucopia of
Chinese esoteric practices
and an organized religion
that is the subsequent
mixture of the two.

3-MINUTE THEOLOGY
Taoism cultivates harmony,
balance, energy, and flow,
as found in nature. Yin
and yang refers to the
mutuality of duality, as
in male and female, dark
and light, hot and cold.
Wu wei, or "non-doing,"
describes the strength
and ease derived from
not resisting present
circumstances, as water
discovers its own level or
a tree develops its own
shape. Taoist appreciation
of simple beauty,
spontaneity, and cryptic
humor informs a Chinese
version of Buddhism: Zen.

The Tao, sometimes translated as
"the way," refers to an omnipresent yet elusive
force or principle that lies at the heart of
everything. Philosophical Taoism, then, is a kind
of engaged mysticism aimed at attuning oneself
with this natural law, typically expressed in the
lives and gnomic utterances of anarchic sages
living in remote bamboo groves. Its core
teachings are found in the Tao Te Ching by
Lao Tzu and the eponymous text of Chuang
Tzu, legendary figures who combine riddlelike
insights into the nature of reality with spiritual
instruction, political counsel, and common
sense. Lao Tzu, for example, says: "Do non-
doing, strive for non-striving." Chuang Tzu
asks: "Am I a man who once dreamed of being
a butterfly, or am I now a butterfly dreaming of
being a man?" Folk Taoism, additionally, refers to
an eclectic range of Chinese lore, including the
worship of local deities, mediumship, divination,
astrology, the aesthetic art of feng shui, the
energy yogas of tai chi and qigong, and alchemy.
Religious Taoism is a systematized combination
of these philosophical and practical strains,
shaped by the example of Mahayana Buddhism,
involving the creation of a literary canon, temple
priestcraft, and monastic orders.

RELATED RELIGIONS
See also
SHENISM
Page 24
MAHAYANA BUDDHISM
Page 40
CONFUCIANISM
Page 50

3-SECOND BIOGRAPHIES
LAO TZU
c.**6th century** BCE

CHUANG TZU
c.**4th century** BCE

SEVEN SAGES OF THE
BAMBOO GROVE
c.**3rd century** CE

30-SECOND TEXT
Alexander Studholme

*Both mystical and
intensely practical,
Taoism sees the natural
flow of the universe
and everything in it.*

CONFUCIANISM
the 30-second religion

Confucius sought to bring

political harmony to times of great social unrest. His teaching had four key themes: mutual consideration, the golden rule of not doing to others what you would not have them do to you; family, encouraging bonds of loyalty, filial piety, and respect for elders; humaneness, expressed in gentlemanly qualities, such as courtesy, generosity, honesty, diligence, and kindness; and ritual, seeing the value of good manners and etiquette, as well as private and public ceremony. Although many people do not regard Confucianism as a religion, his notion of ritual encompassed both the worship of ancestor spirits and the cult of the emperor as the Son of Heaven, a quasi-theistic belief system. In due course, the state encouraged the building of many Confucian temples—including statues of Confucius as a kind of deity—sometimes forcibly replacing Taoist and Buddhist shrines. Until 1905, intimate knowledge of classic texts by Confucius and his disciples formed the basis of Chinese education and the notorious civil service exams. After the Communist revolution, the atheist personality cult of Chairman Mao and his Little Red Book ironically still conformed to the traditional model of a divine emperor and his distribution of Confucian aphorisms.

3-SECOND SERMON
Confucianism is an essentially worldly interpretation of the Tao, "the way," establishing a humane ethical code that shapes Chinese attitudes to family, society, and government.

3-MINUTE THEOLOGY
Confucius comments, for example, on personal morality: "It is shameful to think only of one's salary, whether or not the government accords with the Tao." On education: "A good teacher is one who brings understanding of the new by keeping the old warm." On government: "If one cannot rectify oneself, what business has one rectifying others?" And on human nature: "I have yet to come across anyone who admires virtue as much as sexual attractiveness."

RELATED RELIGIONS
See also
SHENISM
Page 24
MAHAYANA BUDDHISM
Page 40
TAOISM
Page 48

3-SECOND BIOGRAPHIES
CONFUCIUS
C. 551–479 BCE
MENCIUS
C. 371–289 BCE

30-SECOND TEXT
Alexander Studholme

Confucius' moral, philosophical, and political announcements were to assume a quasi-religious significance.

西　東　北

乾　兌　離　震　巽　坎　艮　坤

若へ伏羲の天下に
手ちらし時易と作
らて万民の用ゆと
さんと欲に縫方
遠み作うに天地生
あくくろ死の理も
おくくろ驗ミ家ぞ
ずとりよくろくに
先仰て經緯せん
象を天う觀の八
日月星辰のろろ
盈虧消息の隱見
泄來のなを等の
ふとい心も

I CHING

The basis of the I Ching, a classical Chinese book

of divination, is a set of eight symbols made up of three horizontal lines. Some of the lines are broken (the yin lines), and some are continuous (the yang lines). The eight symbols are known as trigrams; each trigram is named after an aspect of nature (earth, mountain, water, wind, thunder, fire, lake, and heaven) and is given a set of characteristics, such as family relationship, body part, and temperament. Heaven, for instance, is represented by three solid lines and signifies fatherhood, the head, and strength.

So far, so good. But eight symbols don't make for a particularly profound reading, so someone had the idea of combining two trigrams together to create six horizontals lines, known as a hexagram, giving 64 possible combinations. And thus the I Ching was born. On one level, the book can be used as a method of divination. The person asks a question and a set of yarrow stalks (the traditional method) or some coins (the quick method) are cast to create the relevant hexagram. The symbol is then referenced in the I Ching and interpreted accordingly.

The I Ching is much more than a book of clairvoyance. Through the cumulative wisdom of generations of commentators, including no less a figure than Confucius, the text has developed into a philosophy of life. The key themes are pragmatism, rationalism, the balance of opposites, and, central to everything, the inevitability of change. So important is the notion of flux that it is built into the casting of the hexagram, with certain lines changing from yin to yang, and vice versa. According to the I Ching, real wisdom is learning how to deal with that change. Also known as the Book of Change, or the Classic of Change, the I Ching is included as one of the Four Books and Five Classics of Confucianism and is central to both Confucian and Taoist thought.

C.1150 BCE
Wen Wang creates hexagrams, writes Chou I

221 BCE
Survives the burning of the books

551–479 BCE
Ten Wings commentary by Confucius and others

168 BCE
Mawangdui text created, discovered in 1973

C.249 CE
Current order of I Ching established by Wang Bi

A page from the I Ching showing the eight trigrams.

SHINTO

the 30-second religion

3-SECOND SERMON
Shinto is the indigenous
religion of Japan, a
life-affirming animism
calling upon the blessings
of the numinous forces of
nature and of specific
spirit deities.

3-MINUTE THEOLOGY
Shinto is associated with
growth and prosperity,
encouraging people to be
sincere, cheerful, and pure.
Temples host weddings
and blessing ceremonies
for new babies. Priests
conduct groundbreaking
rituals at the start of
building projects and visit
offices at the beginning
of business ventures. The
main festivals are held at
the time of New Year and
the fall harvest. As a result,
Shinto has very little to do
with death: Japanese
funerals are usually
Buddhist affairs.

Shinto understands the world to
be permeated with the presence of *kami*, a
catchall term for invisible spiritual forces that
range from the nameless power that inhabits
a waterfall, beautiful tree, or enigmatic rock
formation, to an actual, personified guardian or
helper. A Shinto religious site can be a formal
temple—approached via a vermilion cross-
beamed gateway—or an unadorned feature
of the Japanese landscape, marked off only by
a white straw rope. The devotee presents an
offering, claps hands or rings a bell to alert the
kami, and says a prayer. Popular *kami* include
Inari, the "carrier of rice," who brings success
in business, and Tenjin, a 9th-century scholar,
to whom students go at exam time. Small *kami*
shrines and amulets are often found in homes
and offices. Shinto celebrates a mythical history
of Japan and the special bond between its
people and its islands. However, in the 19th
century, Shinto was used to legitimize militaristic
and fascist nationalism, a phase that officially
came to an end in 1946, after Japan's defeat
in World War II, when the emperor publicly
renounced the belief that he was a living
embodiment of Amaterasu, the Shinto
goddess of the sun.

RELATED RELIGIONS
See also
ANIMISM
Page 18
MAHAYANA BUDDHISM
Page 40

30-SECOND TEXT
Alexander Studholme

*The animist view of
Shinto celebrates
many aspects of
nature, while praying
to personal deities
brings specific
worldly benefits.*

神道

ABRAHAMIC TRADITIONS

agnostic Someone who is uncertain about the existence (or nonexistence) of God. From the Greek *a* (no) *gnosis* (knowledge), that is, "without knowledge."

asceticism The practice of punishing the body to achieve greater spiritual awareness.

Babism A religion founded in Persia in 1844 by Sayyed 'Ali Mohammad. A mixture of Islam, Christianity, Judaism, and Zoroastrianism, it forbade polygamy, slavery, and alcohol, and advocated a more liberal approach to women's rights. Mohammad adopted the title of the Bab (the Gate) and claimed to be the 12th Imam of the Shi'a tradition. He was executed as a heretic in 1850.

Hadith A collection of sayings and deeds by the prophet Muhammad, based on oral reports, collected together and interpreted by subsequent Islamic scholars. The Hadith is second in authority only to the Qur'an and forms the basis of the Islamic way of life (or Sunna, the tradition of the Prophet).

Halacha The collective rules that govern the Jewish way of life. These are mainly taken from the Torah but also include later traditions and Rabbinic laws. The rules relate to such areas as when and how prayers should be said, how to prepare kosher food, how marital relations should be conducted, and how couples may divorce. The word is derived from the Hebrew for "the path" or "the way of going."

Hasidic A branch of the Jewish religion founded in the 18th century by the Polish rabbi Baal Shem Tov. Its followers believe in a strict interpretation of Jewish law and reject much of modern life, which they see as a distraction from worship.

imam The (male) leader of prayers in an Islamic mosque. The word is also used as a general term of respect for community leaders and teachers. In the Shi'a tradition, the term also refers to the 12 spiritual leaders descended from the Prophet Muhammad.

jihad A struggle or war with a spiritual goal. The term is mainly used in its military sense, as a "holy war" by Muslims against nonbelievers, and has been made famous by the actions of organizations such as Al-Qaida. However, it also refers to an individual's internal struggle for spiritual improvement and the attempt to improve society as a whole.

kosher Food prepared in accordance with Jewish dietary laws.

Mahdi According to some branches of Islam, the Mahdi is a messiah who will appear to redeem humankind before the end of the world. Many people have claimed to be the Mahdi, including Sayyed 'Ali Mohammad, the founder of Babism (see above).

Messiah The savior of the Jews, whose arrival is anticipated in the Old Testament. For Christians, Jesus of Nazareth fulfilled the prophecies and became their Messiah. More generally, the term is used to refer to any savior figure. From the Hebrew word *masiah*, meaning "anointed one."

nomocracy A system of government based on the rule of law—some have described this as encompassing laws formulated by religious leaders. From the Greek *nomos* (law) and *kratia* (to govern).

rabbi A Jewish religious teacher and spiritual leader.

shari'a The codification of the rules and customs governing the Muslim way of life. These are derived both from the Qur'an and the Hadith and apply to religious and secular life. Topics covered include: crime, politics, finance, marital relations, divorce, prayers, fasting, and personal hygiene.

theocracy A system of government based on religious laws. Members of the clergy are usually involved with forming the laws, if not actually applying them. Most theocracies in the West died out during the Enlightenment, with the exception of the Vatican. Elsewhere, Iran is a prominent modern theocracy.

Torah The first five books of the Old Testament—Genesis, Exodus, Leviticus, Numbers, and Deuteronomy—which form the most important part of the Hebrew Bible. According to Jewish tradition, these texts were dictated to Moses by God at Mount Sinai in about 1513 BCE. They contain instructions for every aspect of life set out in 613 commandments (*mitzvot*), which form the basis of the Jewish faith. The best known of these are called the Ten Commandments. The other parts of the Jewish scriptures are Prophets (Nevi'im) and Writings (Keturim).

ORTHODOX JUDAISM

the 30-second religion

Orthodox Judaism is not an organized movement, but a tendency among various groupings focused on resistance to the changes introduced by modernizing factions within the broader Jewish community. It can be traced to mid-19th-century Germany, and characterizes Jews who, countering Reform Judaism, emphasize the unchanging authority of the Torah (Jewish law) and Halacha (interpretations of legal rulings found in holy scripture) contained in the rabbinic texts of the Talmud and Midrash. Orthodox Jews believe God is one and is independent from the world, but has given humankind the law, which reflects the cosmic order God has set in place, so that in following Jewish law and engaging with Halacha, Jews are participating in that order. While more resistant to compromise than Reform and Conservative Jews, the Orthodox often acknowledge the need to engage with the modern world, although the core of Jewish law and tradition are taken to be unchanging. Worldly engagement is seen as particularly problematic by Ultraorthodox or Hasidic Jews, who condemn any deviation from traditional Judaism as they see it, and preserve a sense of purity and difference by maintaining separation from outsiders, wearing distinctive clothing, and adhering to strict rules with regard to food consumption.

RELATED RELIGIONS
See also
REFORM JUDAISM
Page 62

3-SECOND SERMON
Orthodox Judaism is shaped by a resistance to the adaptation of Jewish tradition to the modern age; it prioritizes the preservation of a true or pure Jewish identity.

3-MINUTE THEOLOGY
The relationship between Jewish orthodoxy and the state of Israel is highly complex. The Ultraorthodox Neturei Karta Jews, based in Jerusalem, seek the dismantling of the Jewish state on the grounds that Israel may only be established after the coming of the promised Messiah. The Gush Emunin movement believes it is the religious obligation of Jews to reclaim all land promised to them by God in Genesis 15, whereas, much of the modern-day Zionist movement remains thoroughly secular.

3-SECOND BIOGRAPHIES
ISRAEL BEN ELIEZER
c.1700–1760

MOSHEH SOFER
1762–1839

SAMSON RAPHAEL HIRSCH
1808–1888

30 SECOND TEXT
Mathew Guest

Although recognizing a need to interact with the modern world, Orthodox Jews resist change and view the authority of the Torah as absolute.

REFORM JUDAISM

the 30-second religion

Reform Judaism has its origins in the 18th century, among European Jews who sought to modernize Judaism in keeping with changing times. For some Reform Jews, an unquestioning belief in God comes second to maintaining Judaism as a cultural identity. Some Reform Jews might describe themselves essentially as agnostic, or perhaps willing to reduce Judaism to a kind of ethical monotheism. This radical tendency has proved resilient in the United States, although its breakaway movement of Conservative Judaism—seeking to reconcile elements of traditional Judaism with the realities of life in modern America—is the majority branch. Modernization has taken many forms, including a greater tendency to intermarry with non-Jews, who are welcome at synagogue alongside their partners, and an emphasis on gender equality and freedom of choice. Jewish law is not seen as an unchanging truth, as in Orthodox Judaism, but as a tradition to be used as an adaptable resource. Reform Judaism sees the modern world not as a threat, but as an opportunity to explore more innovative ways of expressing Jewish identity. This includes a commitment to working with other faith groups, including Orthodox Jews and Muslims, and to interfaith dialogue as a way to advance human understanding and harmonious living.

RELATED RELIGIONS
See also
ORTHODOX JUDAISM
Page 60

3-SECOND SERMON
Reform Judaism, a major branch of Jewish religion, is characterized by a commitment to adapt Jewish tradition and identity to the changing norms of modern life.

3-MINUTE THEOLOGY
Reform Jews accord a more limited role than Orthodox Jews to religious ritual, a tendency that can be traced back to the movement's desire to relinquish practices that emphasized the separateness of Jews as a social group, thereby reinforcing its image as a ghetto community. Instead, Reform Judaism has viewed greater cultural integration as a positive means of achieving equal citizenship with the non-Jewish population.

3-SECOND BIOGRAPHIES
MOSES MENDELSSOHN
1729–1786

SAMUEL HOLDHEIM
1806–1860

ABRAHAM GEIGER
1810–1874

I. M. WISE
1819–1900

30-SECOND TEXT
Mathew Guest

Reform Judaism is as much about Jewish culture and identity as it is about Jewish religious practices and beliefs.

וְהִנֵּה בֵּרַכְתָּ בָרֵךְ וַיַּעַן וַיֹּא

ים יְהוָה בְּפִי אֹתוֹ אֶשְׁמֹר לַ

לֵךְ לְךָ נָא אִתִּי אֶל מָקוֹם אַחֵ

פֶס קָצֵהוּ תִרְאֶה וְכֻלּוֹ לֹא תִרְ

וַיִּקָּחֵהוּ שְׂדֵה צֹפִים אֶל רֹ

עָה מִזְבֵּחַ ... פָּר וְאַ

הִתְיַצֵּב ...

יְהוָה

בִלְעָם וַיָּשֶׂם דָב

ת תְּדַבֵּר וַיָּבֹא אֶ

כִּי בָא אֹתוֹ וַיֹּא

יא בִּישִׂיכְלוּ וַיֹּאמֶר

בְּנֵי עָפָר לֹא אִ

חָב הַהוּא אַבִּיר וְ

THE TORAH

The Jewish faith is based on an enormous body
of literature spanning several thousand years. Indeed, the Babylonian
Talmud, which explains and interprets the teachings of the Hebrew
Bible and was collated in the 5th century CE, is some 13,000 pages long.
Then there is the Hebrew Bible itself, which is essentially the Old
Testament part of the Christian Bible and is divided into three parts:
Law (Torah), Prophets (Nevi'im), and Writings (Keturim). At the heart
of this web of learning lies the most important book of all: the Torah,
or the first five books of the Old Testament: Genesis, Exodus, Leviticus,
Numbers, and Deuteronomy. These were the texts that, according to
Jewish tradition, were dictated to Moses by God on Mount Sinai in
about 1513 BCE. They contain instructions for every aspect of life—legal,
ethical, and spiritual—set out in 613 commandments (*mitzvot*), which
form the basis of the Jewish faith. The best known of these are referred
to as the Ten Commandments.

    Copies of the Torah are treated with veneration. The 304,805 letters
of the text are handwritten on parchment by a qualified scribe and can
take up to two years to complete. Once approved, the scroll is kept in an
ark in the wall of a synagogue on the side that faces Jerusalem—and
which the congregation, therefore, faces while praying—and dressed
with a decorated cloth. During services, it is taken out and placed on a
stand (*bimah*) and read using a silver pointer to prevent it from being
soiled by human hand. Every week, a different passage (or *parshah*) of
the Torah is read out and, when the last paragraph of Deuteronomy is
read, the cycle starts again with the first paragraph of Genesis. This
takes a year. Once a scroll is worn out, it is buried in a cemetery.

1513 BCE
Moses speaks to God at
Mount Sinai (apocryphal)

900–450 BCE
Main sections of Hebrew
Bible written

c.90–70 BCE
Council of Jamnia defines
Hebrew Bible
(apocryphal)

1475
First printed edition of
the Torah

1851
First full English
translation of Hebrew
Bible

1917
First Jewish Publication
Society translation

The text of the Torah is written by hand
and can take up to two years to complete.

SUNNI ISLAM

the 30-second religion

Sunna is Arabic for "custom" or "code of behavior," and Sunnis are those who follow the code of behavior established by Muhammad, Allah's final prophet and founder of Islam, as a complement to the teachings of the Qur'an. Sunnis define themselves in terms of practical conformity to Islamic law as agreed by the wider Islamic community to be the authentic practice of the Prophet, who is believed to have led the perfect life. The sunna is embodied in the Hadith, sayings transmitted by the Prophet's followers and interpreted by jurists who then codify it in shari'a, the "way of life" that guides Muslims in all aspects of their daily living. There is no central authority in Sunni Islam, and its teaching emerges from a complex system of jurisprudence—pioneered by al-Shafi'i in the 9th century—which establishes the sunna by deferring to the Qur'an and Hadith alongside the analytical tools of consensus and analogy. The Sunni emphasis on text and law is reflected in its aesthetic traditions. Art featured in mosques is of an entirely abstract character, with no images of created things allowed to distract the mind of the individual Muslim away from the divine word. This is why calligraphy has such a strong and developed tradition in Muslim places of worship.

RELATED RELIGIONS
See also
SHI'A ISLAM
Page 68

3-SECOND BIOGRAPHIES
AL-SHAFI'I
d. 822

ABU AL HASAN AL ASH'ARI
873–935

30-SECOND TEXT
Mathew Guest

3-SECOND SERMON
Sunni Muslims make up the majority group in Islam, defining themselves in terms of their conformity to the tradition of the Prophet Muhammad.

3-MINUTE THEOLOGY
Throughout Sunni history, special status has been accorded to the *ulama*—interpreters of God's word, specialists in classical Arabic, and experts in Qur'anic interpretation. The *ulama* achieved an influential position within Islamic nations, often exerting checks and balances on the power held by dynastic courts. This arrangement has been called a "nomocracy" (from the Greek *nomos*, meaning "law"), because it is based on rule according to God's law, instead of rule by one claiming to be God's representative ("theocracy").

Sunni Muslims are strict adherents to the "way of life" as prescribed in shari'a law, which is in turn defined by authorized lawmakers.

وَإِذْ أَخَذْنَا مِيثَاقَكُمْ لَا تَسْفِكُونَ دِمَاءَكُمْ وَلَا تُخْرِجُونَ
أَنفُسَكُم مِّن دِيَارِكُمْ ثُمَّ أَقْرَرْتُمْ وَأَنتُمْ تَشْهَدُونَ
ثُمَّ أَنتُمْ هَٰؤُلَاءِ تَقْتُلُونَ أَنفُسَكُمْ وَتُخْرِجُونَ فَرِيقًا
مِّنكُم مِّن دِيَارِهِمْ تَظَاهَرُونَ عَلَيْهِم بِالْإِثْمِ وَالْعُدْوَانِ
وَإِن يَأْتُوكُمْ أُسَارَىٰ تُفَادُوهُمْ وَهُوَ مُحَرَّمٌ عَلَيْكُمْ
إِخْرَاجُهُمْ أَفَتُؤْمِنُونَ بِبَعْضِ الْكِتَابِ وَتَكْفُرُونَ بِبَعْضٍ
فَمَا جَزَاءُ مَن يَفْعَلُ ذَٰلِكَ مِنكُمْ إِلَّا خِزْيٌ فِي الْحَيَاةِ الدُّنْيَا
وَيَوْمَ الْقِيَامَةِ يُرَدُّونَ إِلَىٰ أَشَدِّ الْعَذَابِ وَمَا اللَّهُ بِغَافِلٍ
عَمَّا تَعْمَلُونَ ۝ أُولَٰئِكَ الَّذِينَ اشْتَرَوُا الْحَيَاةَ الدُّنْيَا
بِالْآخِرَةِ فَلَا يُخَفَّفُ عَنْهُمُ الْعَذَابُ وَلَا هُمْ يُنصَرُونَ ۝
وَلَقَدْ آتَيْنَا مُوسَى الْكِتَابَ وَقَفَّيْنَا مِن بَعْدِهِ بِالرُّسُلِ
وَآتَيْنَا عِيسَى ابْنَ مَرْيَمَ الْبَيِّنَاتِ وَأَيَّدْنَاهُ بِرُوحِ الْقُدُسِ
أَفَكُلَّمَا جَاءَكُمْ رَسُولٌ بِمَا لَا تَهْوَىٰ أَنفُسُكُمُ اسْتَكْبَرْتُمْ
فَفَرِيقًا كَذَّبْتُمْ وَفَرِيقًا تَقْتُلُونَ ۝ وَقَالُوا قُلُوبُنَا
غُلْفٌ بَل لَّعَنَهُمُ اللَّهُ بِكُفْرِهِمْ فَقَلِيلًا مَّا يُؤْمِنُونَ ۝

SHI'A ISLAM

the 30-second religion

Shi'a Islam takes its name from

the Arabic *shi'at 'Ali*, meaning "party of Ali." Ali was the Prophet Muhmmad's cousin and husband of his daughter Fatima. Those following Ali and his descendants believed themselves to be following the descendants of the Prophet himself, and that these were the rightful leaders of the Muslim community. Shi'a Muslims believe in Allah and the teachings of the Qur'an, but this faction developed its own theology, opposing the majority Sunni view that orthodox teaching was established by consensus among authorized lawmakers; instead, an infallible imam ("leader" or "guide") was believed to be the only source of religious doctrine, with one such imam appearing for each successive generation after Ali himself. Most Shi'a believe the line of imams ended when the 12th Imam, Muhammad al-Muntazar, who mysteriously disappeared in 878. Present-day Shi'a leaders, often called ayatollahs, are seen as caretakers awaiting the return of the 12th imam, who is also sometimes referred to as al-Mahdi, a messianic figure who will triumph over evil and rule over the world at the end of time. Distinctive to the ritual life of Shi'a Islam is the marking of the day Ali's son Husayn was martyred by Umayyad forces in 680. His tomb, in Karbala, Iraq, remains one of the holiest sites for Shi'as outside of Mecca and Medina.

RELATED RELIGIONS
See also
SUNNI ISLAM
Page 66

3-SECOND BIOGRAPHIES
ALI
d. 661

MUHAMMAD AL-MUNTAZAR
d. 878

GRAND AYATOLLAH
RUHOLLAH KHOMEINI
1900–1989

30 SECOND TEXT
Mathew Guest

3-SECOND SERMON
Shi'a is the largest minority branch of Islam, with present-day devotees concentrated in the Persian Gulf region; it diverges from Sunni Islam in its perspectives on authority and leadership.

3-MINUTE THEOLOGY
From the 10th century, Shi'a theology has taken a rationalist character. According to the Shi'a view, the Sunni reliance on learned teachers amounted to mere conjecture, a problem overcome in their deference to the imam. However, after 878, Shi'a were without an imam in the world. The Mu'tazili school of theology provided a solution: *reason* alone provided an authoritative source of teaching, more certain than "tradition," and in keeping with the imam, whose teaching is inevitably an expression of the laws of reason.

Shi'a Islam places much greater emphasis on the bloodline of the Prophet, notably Ali, who along with successive imams, was considered infallible.

THE QUR'AN

To Muslims, the Qur'an is much more than just

a book. It is nothing less than the pure, unadulterated Word of God. For this reason, strict Muslims wash their hands before they open the "Mother of Books" and look after their copies with great care. When the pages are finally worn out, they are not thrown away but placed in a stream to wash away, or buried somewhere remote. Throwing away a copy of the Qur'an or even recycling it is regarded as blasphemy.

According to Muslim belief, the archangel Gabriel revealed the Qur'an to the Prophet Muhammad over a period of 23 years, from 610 CE until his death in 632 CE. Crucially, however, Muhammad did not compose the text himself but merely passed on what was told to him. In this sense, the book differs from the Bible, which is generally accepted as being a human (and, therefore, fallible) account of historical events.

Yet the Qur'an was never committed to paper during Muhammad's lifetime. Instead, it was memorized by thousands of his followers, with fragments of it written on palm leaves, flat stones, and even bones. After Muhammad's death, the first caliph Abu Bakr collected all the verses together and put them in a book, which he entrusted to Muhammad's widow Hafsa. Within a few years, however, regional variations started creeping into the text, so the third caliph Uthman reissued copies of Hafsa's book and had all other versions burned. This so-called "Uthmanic recension" forms the basis of today's book.

The authenticity of the text is important to Muslims, who memorize verses and use them in prayer. A few exceptional individuals, known as hafiz, memorize the entire text—114 chapters, 6,236 verses, and, when translated into English, some 78,000 words.

610
Text is revealed to Muhammad

632
Muhammad dies

c.650
Caliph Uthman issues standardized version

c.1143
First non-Arabic (Latin) translation

1649
First English translation

1935
Egypt issues standardized version

The first page of the Holy Qur'an—copies are treated with the utmost respect.

SUFISM

the 30-second religion

3-SECOND SERMON
The mystical branch of Islam, Sufism focuses on the quest for knowledge of God realized in a series of inner states or experiences.

3-MINUTE THEOLOGY
Some Sufis have made sense of their connection with the divine as an actual union with God. The sayings of 9th-century mystic Abu Yazid al Bistami often feature a shift in voice from the third to the first person—Abu Yazid addressing his readers as if he were God. While the Qur'an portrays Muhammad using this same practice, the suggestion that mystical experience leads to an identification with the divine remained controversial, especially among the *ulama* ("lawgivers") of orthodox Islam.

Originally influenced by the ascetics of the Eastern Christian tradition, Sufis emphasized the importance of renunciation of worldly things, a celebration of poverty and inner purity. Unlike in Christian monasticism, however, these were not justified in terms of the need to mortify the flesh, but as a liberation of the human spirit as a means of achieving a greater intimacy with God. Sufis have been controversial in the history of Islam, not least because their emphasis on the "inner life" has been interpreted as a rejection of the outward observance codified in shari'a law and in ritual observance such as daily prayer. The 11th-century Persian theologian Al-Ghazali is renowned in part because he sought a "middle way" between the pious theology of shari'a and the experiential devotion to God affirmed by Sufism. While mainstream orthodox Islam tends to frown upon the use of music in worship, Sufis have a long tradition of using music and dance for devotional purposes. Probably the most celebrated example are the so-called "whirling dervishes" of the Turkish Mevlevi order—now witnessed primarily as a tourist attraction—whose dance emulates the revolution of the planets around the sun.

RELATED RELIGIONS
See also
SUNNI ISLAM
Page 66

SHI'A ISLAM
Page 68

3-SECOND BIOGRAPHIES
MANSUR AL-HALLAJ
c.858–922

AL-GHAZALI
1058–1111

30-SECOND TEXT
Mathew Guest

Often thought of as the mystical branch of Islam, Sufism espouses asceticism as a means of getting closer to God.

AHMADIYYA

the 30-second religion

The Ahmadiyya movement was
founded in India in 1889 by Mirza Ghulam
Ahmad, who believed himself to be the
promised Messiah, or Mahdi, for the Muslim
community. At various times, Ahmad also
claimed to be the Mujaddid, or "renewer," of
Islam, an avatar of the Hindu god Krishna, the
returned Jesus, and a manifestation of the
Prophet Muhammad. While consistently
maintaining that a chief goal is to revitalize
Islam, Ahmadis are generally viewed as suspect
by orthodox Muslims. While Ahmad maintained
that he was subordinate to Muhammad, his
claim to deliver a new revelation of God's
teaching, intended to return Islam to its proper
state, sat uncomfortably with Islam's central
tenet that Muhammad is the "seal" of the
prophets. Indeed, this has led to some
persecution of the Ahmadiyya in Muslim
countries, such as Pakistan, in which it has been
declared a "non-Muslim minority." Ahmadis
retain a primary place for the teaching of
Ahmad alongside the Qur'an, and this includes
a call for the end of religious wars and the
institution of peace and social justice. Like
the Baha'i, Ahmadis recognize the teachings
of other religious founders, including Zoroaster,
Buddha, and Confucius, but Ahmad taught
that these converge in the one true Islam.

3-SECOND SERMON
The Ahmadiyya is a
revivalist movement within
Islam, which breaks from
Islamic orthodoxy in its
adherence to the teachings
of a messianic leader.

3-MINUTE THEOLOGY
The Ahmadiyya movement
has a fervent global
missionary program that
seeks the promotion of
Islam through peaceful
means, especially the
propagation of literature
and translation of the
Qur'an into numerous
languages. In this sense,
the movement stresses
the interpretation of jihad
as primarily a struggle
against one's own base
desires. Following Ahmad's
teaching, the concept of
violent jihad (holy war) is
viewed as unnecessary in
modern times—the right
response to hate being
love and kindness.

3-SECOND BIOGRAPHIES
MIRZA GHULAM AHMAD
1835–1908

MAULANA HAKEEM
NOOR-UD-DIN
1841–1914

MUHAMMAD ABDUS SALAM
1926–1996

30 SECOND TEXT
Mathew Guest

*Often shunned by
orthodox Muslims, the
Ahmadiyya community
are supporters of the
self-proclaimed
Messiah and prophet
Mirza Ghulam Ahmad.*

BAHA'I FAITH

the 30-second religion

Baha'ism originated in Iran in the 1860s as a movement within Babism, which in turn was a sect within Shi'a Islam. Its founder, Bahá'u'lláh, believed himself to be a prophet with a new set of revelations, conceived as emerging within a long line of successive prophets including Abraham and Jesus. Originally confined to the Middle East, Baha'ism expanded into the United States in 1894, and found the religious diversity there well suited to its ambitions to break away from Shi'a Islam altogether—instead proclaiming itself as a new world faith, at once the successor and culmination of all world religions. Baha'is are distinctive in remaining committed to its global mission (especially in the developing world), while affirming radically inclusive values, including the oneness of humanity, universal education, the harmony of religion and science, monogamy, and equality of the sexes. The movement also exists without a strict hierarchy or priesthood, although it has a rationalized administrative structure and views Bahá'u'lláh and his writings as manifestations of divinity. Baha'is gather together on a local basis for prayer, sacred readings, and for shared food and communal activities organized by locally elected assemblies.

RELATED RELIGIONS
See also
SHI'A ISLAM
Page 68

3-SECOND SERMON
Central to Baha'ism is a conviction of the essential unity of all religious faiths, reflecting its emphasis on celebrating humanity and seeking world peace.

3-MINUTE THEOLOGY
While it has its theological roots firmly in 19th-century Iranian Shi'a Islam, Baha'ism has been most radically shaped over the past 100 years by its encounter with Western culture. Expanding through the West, it has developed ideals of global unity that dovetail with values associated with transnational organizations, such as the United Nations. However, the Baha'i vision of unity is not based on democracy as such, but on what it sees as universal principles of morality.

3-SECOND BIOGRAPHIES
BAHÁ'U'LLÁH
1817–1892

'ABD AL-BAHA
1844–1921

SHOGHI EFFENDI
1897–1957

30-SECOND TEXT
Mathew Guest

Expanding from its Shi'a Islam ancestry, Baha'ism promotes itself as a global faith with religious unity, world peace, and equality at its core.

EUROPEAN CHRISTIANITIES

EUROPEAN CHRISTIANITIES
GLOSSARY

Assumption The taking of Mary's body to heaven after her death, also known as the Dormition (falling asleep). Celebrated by Roman Catholics for hundreds of year, with the feast of the Assumption on August 15, it was only made part of Catholic dogma by Pope Pius XII in 1950.

elect According to Calvinism, those preselected by God for salvation.

Eucharist A Christian ceremony that commemorates the meal Christ shared with his disciples before being crucified. The Last Supper is reenacted through drinking wine (or grape juice) and eating bread. Although all Christians celebrate the Eucharist, they differ in their interpretation of it, with Catholics believing the bread and wine are the actual body and blood of Christ, while Protestants take a less literal approach.

evangelical Belonging to a form of Christianity that seeks to return to the basic tenets of the New Testament, instead of later interpretations. The movement started with the teachings of Martin Luther, John Calvin, and Ulrich Zwingli in the 16th century but has since been adopted by many other fundamentalist churches.

excommunicated To be excluded from a church or religious community.

Fall, The In Christian mythology, this is the moment humankind lost its innocence and committed its first sin. Despite being told by God not to eat the fruit from the Tree of Knowledge, Adam and Eve succumb to temptation, whereupon they become ashamed of their nakedness and are expelled from paradise.

First Great Awakening A revival of religious piety that took place in the Americas in the mid-18th century. The movement was inspired by powerful evangelical sermons by charismatic preachers, which appealed to people's personal guilt. Starting in Pennsylvania and New Jersey, the movement was spread throughout the Americas by missionaries. The Second Great Awakening was a similar movement that took place in the early 19th century.

Gospel The first books of the New Testament, named after Jesus' followers Matthew, Mark, Luke, and John, traditionally considered to be their authors. Gospel also refers to Jesus' message, or the "good news" of salvation. The word itself comes from the Old English *godspel*, meaning "good tidings."

Great Schism The splitting of the Christian Church into the Roman Catholic and Greek Orthodox factions in 1054 (also known as the East–West Schism). The separation occurred for a number of reasons, including the refusal of the Greek-speaking Catholics to recognize Rome as the primary authority for their faith. There was also disagreement about the formation of the Holy Spirit and whether the bread at communion should be leaven or unleaven.

icons Figures or paintings of sacred figures, such as Christian saints, venerated in certain religions.

Immaculate Conception The idea that Mary, mother of Christ, was conceived without sin. This is different from the virgin birth, which suggests that Mary gave birth to Christ while remaining a virgin throughout.

indulgence The forgiving of a sin and remission from punishment. In the Middle Ages, indulgences were given out by the Catholic Church as a reward for good deeds and devout behavior. However, the system was increasingly abused, with professional "pardoners" raising funds for the Church (and themselves) through the sale of indulgences.

predestination The theory that God has decided the outcome of all things into infinity, including who will be saved. Calvinists extend the idea further and believe in "double-predestination," that God has predetermined who will be saved and who will be left to suffer eternal damnation for their sins.

Reformation A movement in 16th-century Europe that attempted to reform the Catholic Church and rid it of corrupt practices, such as the sale of indulgences. It began with the publication of Martin Luther's *The Ninety-Five Theses* in 1517, and lead to the dissolutions of monasteries in England and the creation of the Protestant churches.

sacrament A religious ceremony thought to bestow a blessing on those who take part. The Protestant Church recognizes two sacraments, baptism and Holy Communion, while the Catholic Church has seven: baptism, confirmation, confession, marriage, ordination, Holy Communion, and Last Rites.

Tree of Knowledge A tree in the Garden of Eden from which Adam and Eve were forbidden to eat. Their failure to obey God's word was, according to Christian belief, humanity's original sin.

ROMAN CATHOLICISM

the 30-second religion

The Roman Catholic Church is
the largest unified religious organization in the
world—over half the world's Christians are
Catholics. The head of the Church is the Bishop
of Rome (known as the Pope from the informal
Greek term *pappas* for "father"), who claims
unbroken succession from Saint Peter, the first
Bishop of Rome and designated leader of Jesus'
followers. The Catholic Church considers its
primary purpose is to proclaim the good news
(Gospel) of Jesus Christ, namely that God
has saved the world from its state of sin
by becoming incarnate in the man Jesus of
Nazareth. For Catholics, the Church itself is the
continuing presence on earth of Jesus, ensuring
that God's work of salvation is maintained
until Jesus' prophesized return. Sacraments
are central to the Catholic Church's work,
understood as visible signs of God's grace
entrusted to the Church. The principal
sacrament is the Eucharist, in which bread and
wine are believed to be transformed into Jesus'
body and blood. Catholics believe that after
death each person's soul is judged: the virtuous
unite with God in heaven; the wicked are
separated from God in hell; the rest find
purgatory, a temporary state of cleansing
before admission to heaven.

RELATED RELIGIONS
See also
ABRAHAMIC TRADITIONS
Pages 56–77
EUROPEAN CHRISTIANITIES
Pages 78–97
WORLD CHRISTIANITIES
Pages 98–115

3-SECOND BIOGRAPHIES
JESUS
C.5 BCE– C.30 CE

SAINT PETER
C.1 BCE–67 CE

THOMAS AQUINAS
1225–1274

30-SECOND TEXT
Russell Re Manning

3-SECOND SERMON
The largest Christian
denomination, headed
by the Pope and with a
mission to spread the
good news (Gospel) of
Jesus Christ, administer
the sacraments, and
exercise charity.

3-MINUTE THEOLOGY
For Catholics, Jesus'
mother, Mary, is a figure
of widespread popular
veneration. Catholics
believe Mary was
conceived without sin
("Immaculate Conception"),
that she herself conceived
Jesus miraculously through
the agency of the Holy
Spirit ("virgin birth"), and
that at the end of her
earthly life she was taken
up to heaven body and
soul ("Assumption"). Many
important Catholic shrines
are associated with
miraculous appearances
of Mary, notably, at
Guadalupe, Fatima,
and Lourdes.

*Mary plays a much
more significant role
in Catholicism than in
any other Christian
Church—the image of
the Madonna and Child
is notably widespread.*

EASTERN ORTHODOXY

the 30-second religion

The Eastern Orthodox Church is

a collection of at least 14 self-governing churches, united theologically yet without a centralized institutional structure. Orthodox Christians believe their Church has an unbroken link back to the first church founded by Saint Paul and represents the original expression of Christian doctrine as it was developed in the eastern Mediterranean. Associated with the Byzantine Empire, the Orthodox Church split from the Roman Catholic Church for doctrinal and political reasons; officially the Great Schism (1054) was caused by theological disagreements about the doctrine of the Holy Spirit (the *Filioque* debate), but in practice political differences between Constantinople and Rome also played their part. Orthodox Christians consider religious life as a form of *theosis* (literally "becoming divine"), in which the believer is spiritually transformed through a process of a mystical identification with Jesus Christ. Prayer and contemplation of the mysteries of faith are central to this form of life, of which monasticism is an ideal example. Eastern Orthodoxy believes Jesus' Resurrection from the dead after three days to be the central mystery of Christianity, which gives hope in the final victory of God through Jesus, which is often represented in the figure of the *Christ pantocrator* (literally "all-powerful").

3-SECOND SERMON
A communion of self-governing Christian churches across eastern Europe and the eastern Mediterranean that is characterized by practices of spiritual transformation and the use of icons.

3-MINUTE THEOLOGY
Icons (*eikona*) are fundamental to Eastern Orthodox worship. These highly stylized images of Jesus, Mary, and the saints are found in abundance in churches, in particular on the large screen (*iconostasis*) that separates the nave from the sanctuary, and in believers' homes. Orthodox Christians do not worship the icons, but rather venerate them as images of the archetype they represent, just as Christ himself is believed to be the visible incarnation of the invisible God.

RELATED RELIGIONS
See also
ABRAHAMIC TRADITIONS
Pages 56–77
EUROPEAN CHRISTIANITIES
Pages 78–97
WORLD CHRISTIANITIES
Pages 98–115

3-SECOND BIOGRAPHY
JESUS
C.5 BCE– C.30 CE

PHOTIUS I
c.810–c.893

GREGORY PALAMAS
1296–1359

MARK OF EPHESUS
1392–1444

30-SECOND TEXT
Russell Re Manning

Eastern Orthodoxy views the Holy Spirit to proceed from the Father alone, and not also from the Son—the Filioque debate that split East and West.

THE BIBLE

The "best-selling book of all time," the Bible is
estimated to have sold between 2.5 and 6 billion copies, depending
on your source. Yet the Christian holy book is an unlikely mix of texts
written by 40 authors in three languages over the space of 1,500
years. And what's more, there are many different versions available.

In terms of structure, the Bible is made up of two parts. The first
part, the Old Testament, written between 1200 and 165 BCE, consists of
39 books and covers the history of the world from its creation (Genesis)
up until shortly before the birth of Jesus Christ. This is by far the longer
of the two parts. The New Testament, written in the first century CE,
consists of 27 books describing the life of Jesus and the origins of
Christianity. There are the gospels of Matthew, Mark, Luke, and John,
followed by an account of the first 30 years of Christianity (Acts) written
by Luke, followed in turn by 21 pastoral letters (or epistles) written by
Paul and others, and finally the apocalyptic vision of Revelation.

Although written by different people and for different audiences, the
four gospels (from the Old English *godspel*, meaning "good news") broadly
agree on the main events in Jesus' life. Matthew and John are both said to
have known Jesus personally, while Mark and Luke were closely connected
to the apostles, and all the accounts were written within 70 years of
Christ's Crucifixion. The letters, on the other hand, were written by Church
leaders to their disciples and, with the exception of Romans and Hebrews,
were not intended to officially represent Christian doctrine. As such,
they are more conversational and sometimes sound like one side of a
dialogue, or as answers to questions submitted by disciples.

Favorite sections (such as John 3:16) have been translated into
3,000 languages, while the Bible itself is available in 400. Despite
such a diverse literal provenance, to devout Christians the book is
"divinely inspired," and, therefore, the work of just one author: God.

The Bible is the sacred book of Christianity,
comprising the Old and New Testaments.

C.450 BCE
Hebrew Bible (*Tanakh*)
created

C.250 BCE
Hebrew Bible translated
into Greek

C.200 CE
New Testament
translated into Latin

1456
Gutenberg Bible, first
printed edition

1534
Luther Bible, first full
translation into German

1535
Coverdale Bible, first full
translation into English

1558
Geneva version
introduces verse numbers

1611
Authorized King James
version

LUTHERANISM
the 30-second religion

In 1517, Martin Luther, a priest
and theologian in Wittenberg, Germany,
protested against the Catholic Church's practice
of selling "indulgences," which promised believers
remission of sin in exchange for financial
donations. Luther affirmed that only God could
grant forgiveness from sin. In the context of
widespread dissatisfaction with the established
Church and aided by the recently invented
printing press, Luther's ideas spread rapidly,
leading to the religious and political upheavals
of the Protestant Reformation. Luther's concept
of justification by grace through faith alone
rejects all human attempts to gain God's favor,
and hence grace, as the idolatrous works of sin;
instead Lutherans rely on God's initiative in Jesus
Christ as the only means to salvation. Luther
derived this doctrine from a close study of
the Bible, which he translated from Latin into
vernacular German and which Lutherans hold
as normative for all subsequent religious
thought and practice. Lutherans stress the
importance of the individual believer's personal
faith, with some followers, known as "pietists"
(from the word "piety"), emphasizing the
emotional and subjective elements of belief.
While Lutheran worship retains the centrality
of the Eucharist, a significant role is given to
the Scriptures and to inclusive participation,
especially communal singing.

3-SECOND SERMON
A branch of Protestant
Christianity inspired by the
teachings of the reformer
Martin Luther, based on
the idea of justification by
grace through faith alone.

3-MINUTE THEOLOGY
Luther reacted to what
he saw as the "cult" of
the saints in Roman
Catholicism, affirming
instead that Christians
should have no other
mediator than Christ
himself. As a result,
Lutherans do not venerate
the saints as intercessors
but honor them as
examples of pure faith
and divine mercy. Similarly,
many Lutherans pray to
the Virgin Mary for God
to do what they ask
through her, but insist that
the work is God's alone.

RELATED RELIGIONS
See also
ABRAHAMIC TRADITIONS
Pages 56–77
EUROPEAN CHRISTIANITIES
Pages 78–97
WORLD CHRISTIANITIES
Pages 98–115

3-SECOND BIOGRAPHIES
JESUS
C.5 BCE– C.30 CE

MARTIN LUTHER
1483–1546

30-SECOND TEXT
Russell Re Manning

Luther's posting of the
Ninety-Five Theses on a
church in Wittenberg,
questioning the validity
of indulgences, is
widely seen as the start
of the Reformation.

CALVINISM

the 30-second religion

John Calvin was a Protestant

thinker who developed the "reform" of Christianity begun by Martin Luther. Today, over 75 million "Reformed" Christians share the principles of his theological system. Calvinism teaches the absolute sovereignty of God and the total depravity (original sin) of humanity. As a consequence of the Fall (Adam and Eve's disobedience of God's command not to eat from the "Tree of Knowledge"), all people are in every respect enslaved to sin and, hence, incapable of being moral without external agency. For Calvinists, God, who would be justified in condemning all humanity, instead voluntarily decides to be merciful to some. Calvinists believe that these elect are saved because of God's free irresistible grace, not because of any virtue or quality they possess. Only the elect are saved and preserved forever in communion with God through his grace alone; all others are condemned. Calvinism holds that only practices that are instituted in the New Testament should have a place in Christian worship ("the regulative principle"), leading to the widespread rejection of all visual images in churches and their replacement with texts, such as the Ten Commandments, although recently hymns and "worship songs" have become more common.

3-SECOND SERMON
The "Five Points" of Calvinism affirm belief in total depravity, unconditional election, limited atonement, irresistible grace, and preservation of the saints.

3-MINUTE THEOLOGY
Predestination is the Calvinist belief in God's free choice to save some people, leaving the remainder to suffer (deservedly) eternal damnation for their sins. Some Calvinists believe that God ordained who would be saved before the event of the Fall ("supralapsarianism"), others that God's election occurred after the Fall ("intralapsarianism") because salvation logically requires something to be saved from. "Double predestination" is the view that God elects both whom to save and whom to damn.

RELATED RELIGIONS
See also
ABRAHAMIC TRADITIONS
Pages 56–77
EUROPEAN CHRISTIANITIES
Pages 78–97
WORLD CHRISTIANITIES
Pages 98–115

3-SECOND BIOGRAPHIES
JESUS
C.5 BCE– C.30 CE

JOHN CALVIN
1509–1564

30-SECOND TEXT
Russell Re Manning

For Calvinists, God's rule is absolute, and only through his grace and mercy will the elect be saved.

ANGLICANISM (EPISCOPALIANISM)

the 30-second religion

RELATED RELIGIONS
See also
ORTHODOX JUDAISM
Page 60
EUROPEAN CHRISTIANITIES
Pages 78–97
WORLD CHRISTIANITIES
Pages 98–115

3-SECOND SERMON
The religious beliefs of a global collection of churches, the history of which can be traced back to the post-Reformation Church of England.

3-MINUTE THEOLOGY
As with many Christian Churches, the status of women in the Anglican Communion is controversial. Most Anglican provinces ordain women as priests and some permit the ordination of women as bishops. For many, the issue is one of equality under God; for others, the ambiguity of the Biblical view is crucial, for example, Galatians 3:24 asserts that gender is surpassed in Christianity, while the epistle 1 Timothy subordinates women to men and requires that women stay silent in worship.

In 1521, King Henry VIII of England was granted the title "Defender of the Faith" (*fidei defensor*) by Pope Leo X for his pamphlet accusing Martin Luther of heresy. Thirteen years later, an Act of Parliament declared an excommunicated Henry "the only supreme head on earth of the Church in England." The unusual historical origins of the Church of England—part religious renewal, part royal love story, part *Realpolitik*—define the characteristics of Anglicanism as a Protestant Christian tradition. The wider Anglican Communion is made up of 44 provinces, including the Episcopal Church of the United States, united by the Archbishop of Canterbury—known as the *primus inter pares*, or first among equals. Within the Anglican Communion there is a very wide range of beliefs and practices. For "evangelical" Anglicans, the reformed emphasis on the Bible is central; for "Anglo-Catholics," the focus is rather on religious liturgy and the continuity of the Anglican Church with its pre-Reformation origins. Richard Hooker's account of the so-called "three-legged stool" of Anglican beliefs—derived primarily from the scriptures, informed by reason, and supported by tradition—has been an influential statement of the nature of Anglican authority.

3-SECOND BIOGRAPHIES
JESUS
c.5 BCE–c.30 CE

HENRY VIII
1491–1547

RICHARD HOOKER
1554–1600

ROWAN WILLIAMS
1950–

30-SECOND TEXT
Russell Re Manning

The 44 regional and national member churches of the Anglican Communion affirm their beliefs through the Anglican Communion Covenant.

METHODISM

the 30-second religion

3-SECOND SERMON
Revivalist movement
originating within
Anglicanism that stresses
the need for personal piety
and individual good works
in response to God's grace.

3-MINUTE THEOLOGY
Methodists were central
figures in the so-called
First Great Awakening in
America in the 1730s and
1740s. This religious
revivalist movement had
a profound effect on the
future of religious belief in
the Americas, encouraging
a skepticism toward ritual
and established religious
traditions and emphasizing
instead the importance
of personal faith and
individual good works.
The most famous itinerant
Methodist preacher was
George Whitefield, whose
enthusiastic sermons
attracted large crowds
and resulted in mass
conversions.

Methodists were so-named on account of the highly methodological habits of a group of students who met in Oxford, England, in the 1730s for the purposes of mutual improvement. Among their disciplines were regular communion and fasting, abstinence from amusement and luxuries, as well as frequent missions to the poor. Developed from the teachings of the Anglican priest John Wesley and his younger brother Charles, Methodism is characterized by its emphasis on the importance of the spiritual transformation of the individual through close study of the Christian Scriptures, and through practical action to promote social welfare and justice. Methodists were prominent antislavery campaigners, were frequently active promoters of the temperance movement, and strove to spread their message overseas through extensive missionary activity. The Methodist interest in social matters is reflected in their practice of preaching outside churches, taking the Gospel to the "unchurched" in market places and prisons. Methodist churches often have an annual Covenant Service on the first Sunday of the year, in which believers reaffirm their total reliance on God and their willingness to devote themselves to His service.

RELATED RELIGIONS
See also
ORTHODOX JUDAISM
Page 60
EUROPEAN CHRISTIANITIES
Pages 78–97
WORLD CHRISTIANITIES
Pages 98–115

3-SECOND BIOGRAPHIES
JESUS
C.5 BCE–C.30 CE

JOHN WESLEY
1703–1791

CHARLES WESLEY
1707–1788

30-SECOND TEXT
Russell Re Manning

Morality and social welfare are central to Methodist practice. Methodism founder John Wesley was an active campaigner against slavery and discouraged the drinking of alcohol.

SOCIETY OF FRIENDS (QUAKERS)

the 30-second religion

In 1650, the Christian dissenter George Fox, on trial for blasphemy, exhorted the judge to "tremble at the word of the Lord." The judge found Fox guilty, sent him to prison, and mocked him as a "quaker"—a name that was soon adopted by groups of nonconformist Christian revivalists—otherwise known as "Children of the Light," "Friends of Truth," or the "Society of Friends." Quakers believe that a direct experience of God through Christ is available to all people—without the intervention of clergy—and that through "the inner light" God is always present to all people, without the mediation of religious sacraments. As a result, although most Quakers hold regular services of worship, they are known as meetings and are often "unprogrammed," with no designated leader or predetermined structure. Sometimes worshippers take turns to speak when they feel led by the Holy Spirit, but frequently the entire meeting takes place in silence because believers gather simply to wait "expectantly" in the presence of God and their fellows. It is important for most Quakers to bear witness or "testify" to their faith in their everyday actions, which aim to embody the values of peace, equality, simplicity, and truth.

3-SECOND SERMON
A Christian dissenting movement that rejects religious hierarchy and institutions in favor of an unmediated experience of God.

3-MINUTE THEOLOGY
Quakers are committed to promoting peace and are strongly opposed to all forms of violence and armed conflict. They derive their pacifism from Jesus' command "to love your enemies" and their belief in the inner light of God. Quakers "conscientiously" object to conscription to armed forces and many refuse to pay that portion of their taxes that is to be spent on weapons. In 1947, the Society of Friends was awarded the Nobel Peace Prize.

RELATED RELIGIONS
See also
ORTHODOX JUDAISM
Page 60
EUROPEAN CHRISTIANITIES
Pages 78–97
WORLD CHRISTIANITIES
Pages 98–115

3-SECOND BIOGRAPHIES
JESUS
C.5 BCE–C.30 CE
GEORGE FOX
1624–1691

30-SECOND TEXT
Russell Re Manning

Quakers believe that the inner light of God exists in every man and every woman; as such, everyone shall be considered equal.

WORLD CHRISTIANITIES

baptism A Christian ceremony during which a person is immersed in or sprinkled with water as part of their initiation into the faith. The act is intended to symbolize the cleansing of the soul. Most Christian churches insist on the baptism of children, but not necessarily of adults.

credobaptism The baptism of someone who has affirmed their belief in the Christian faith. This contrasts with the baptism of children (known as pedobaptism), during which an affirmation of belief is not required. Some Christian churches believe that only the baptism of consenting adults is valid; full immersion in water is often required as part of the ceremony.

millenarianism The belief that a major catastrophe or apocalypse is imminent. This is often linked to the belief that the world is being ruled by corrupt or evil forces, which must be overthrown in order for the true faith to prevail. Millenarianists include Christians who believe in the second coming of Christ.

monasticism The religious practice of abandoning mainstream society and devoting one's life to spiritual development and prayer. Derived from the Greek *monos*, meaning "only one, alone." Many faiths have strong monastic traditions, including Christianity, Buddhism, and Hinduism.

pedobaptism The baptism of children, where an affirmation of belief is not required, as opposed to credobaptism (the baptism of adults), where it is.

Pentecost A Christian festival that celebrates the descent of the Holy Spirit among Christ's disciples 50 days after his death (hence Pentecost, from the Greek for "fifty days"). According to the Bible, after the Holy Spirit had descended, the disciples started to "speak in tongues" and were understood by those present, each in their own language. This led to the creation of the Christian Church.

Rapture The idea that Jesus will reappear in the sky and that all true believers will rise up to meet him. There is some disagreement about when this will happen, however, with some believing it has already happened, during the destruction of Jerusalem in 70 CE, as described in Matthew 24.

repentance The regret of past misdeeds and commitment to change one's behavior in the future. In a religious context, this usually means showing contrition for not obeying the rules of the faith and reaffirming belief in that faith.

Resurrection The return to life of a dead body. According to Christian belief, Christ came back to life three days after his body was placed in a tomb. The Resurrection is one of the central tenets of the Christian faith, because it symbolizes the possibility of redemption for all believers after they die. Indeed, a passage from the Bible says: "If Christ be not risen, then is our preaching vain" (1 Corinthians 15:14).

Sabbath A day of rest and worship in Judeo-Christian religions. According to Genesis, God created the world in six days and rested on the seventh. However, not everyone agrees which day it was, with most Jews observing the Sabbath on Saturday, while most Christians observe it on Sunday.

speaking in tongues Uttering noises that sound like language but have no known meaning. The speaker usually makes the sounds while in a trance and, according to certain religious groups, is possessed by a supernatural force. Also known as "glossolalia."

spiritual warfare The belief that the will of God is constantly under attack from the forces of evil. This can take many forms, from the thwarting of religious works through to people being possessed by the devil. Several evangelical churches promote this idea and practice different ways of casting out demons from those thought to be affected.

Trinity The idea that God exists in three persons, the Father, the Son, and the Holy Spirit, who are essentially one. This is a central tenet of the Christian faith, although its exact formulation is disputed and was one of the reasons the Orthodox Greek Church split from the Roman Catholic Church in 1054.

COPTIC CHRISTIANITY

the 30-second religion

In 451 CE, Anatolius, the Patriarch of Constantinople, convened the Council of Chalcedon in an attempt to settle theological controversy about the nature of Jesus Christ. The Council affirmed Jesus as "fully human and fully divine": two natures united in one person. Not all agreed, with the "oriental orthodox" bishops believing instead that Jesus is of one nature: one nature consisting of humanity and divinity. The difference may seem slight, but it was enough to trigger the first major schism within Christianity and the result was the Coptic Orthodox Church of Alexandria. Even before Chalcedon, Christianity in Egypt had taken a distinctive form, using the local language of Coptic (instead of Greek or Latin) and adopting practices of desert monasticism. The writings of the Desert Fathers, especially their sermons, are highly influential for Coptic Christian spirituality, in particular, the tradition of *hesychasm* (from the Greek for "stillness"), which promotes the practice of "interior silence and continual prayer." Copts use a liturgical calendar, based on ancient Egyptian traditions, consisting of 13 months and three seasons: inundation, sowing, and harvest. The head of the Coptic Church is the Pope of Alexandria (presently Shenouda III), believed to be a successor to the Apostle Mark, who founded the first church in Egypt.

3-SECOND SERMON
Ancient Christian Church based in Egypt, born out of a Christological schism and the cradle of Christian monasticism.

3-MINUTE THEOLOGY
While monasticism is widespread in religious traditions, Christian monastic practices are widely held to originate with the communities and individuals who isolated themselves from worldly life in the Egyptian deserts and inspired the ascetic spirituality of the Coptic Church. Following in the footsteps of Saint Anthony, Coptic monastic traditions emphasize practices of withdrawal and abstention—sometimes to complete isolation and silence—to enable believers to devote themselves fully to a life of prayer and contemplation.

RELATED RELIGIONS
See also
ORTHODOX JUDAISM
Page 60
EUROPEAN CHRISTIANITIES
Pages 78–97
WORLD CHRISTIANITIES
Pages 98–115

3-SECOND BIOGRAPHIES
JESUS
C.5 BCE–C.30 CE

SHENOUDA III
1923–

30-SECOND TEXT
Russell Re Manning

Coptic Christianity's practice of desert asceticism is regarded as the precursor of Christian monasticism.

PENTECOSTALISM

the 30-second religion

Pentecostalism takes its name

from the Christian festival of Pentecost, which commemorates the episode after Jesus' death and Resurrection when his disciples were filled with the Holy Spirit of God and spoke in tongues (strange utterances interpreted as unknown or divine language). This phenomenon was recognized in the early Church as a sign of God's presence, although later the Church came to view these episodes as ceasing with the death of the first disciples (the "cessationist" perspective). Things changed at the turn of the 20th century, when groups of North American Christians began to experience what they viewed as the Holy Spirit, and again spoke in tongues as an expression of this. Most influential was the Azusa St. Revival in Los Angeles in 1906, led by African-American preacher William Joseph Seymour, notable for spanning the racial divide. Devotees united in their experience of the Spirit, which initially overruled any notion of hierarchy, priesthood, or privilege. Pentecostals continue to speak in tongues and some see this as a sign of their salvation as Christians. Others view it as "second blessing," a confirmation of being one of God's people following the initiation of baptism. Pentecostalism is the fastest-growing branch of Christianity, making up well over a quarter of all Christians.

3-SECOND SERMON
A branch of Christianity centered on a belief in the present-day reality of spiritual gifts bestowed by the Holy Spirit.

3-MINUTE THEOLOGY
Some Pentecostals believe in "spiritual warfare," which refers to the struggle Christians are called to in battling evil powers with the power of God. This is expressed in praying over those thought to be possessed by demons, calling upon God to heal the sick. This reflects a "restorationist" dimension; Pentecostals see themselves as restoring the Church to its original form, when Christians drove out demons and healed the sick, following Jesus' example.

RELATED RELIGIONS
See also
LUTHERANISM
Page 88
BAPTIST CHRISTIANITY
Page 110

3-SECOND BIOGRAPHY
WILLIAM J. SEYMOUR
1870–1922

30-SECOND TEXT
Mathew Guest

Pentecostals firmly believe in the presence of the Holy Spirit of God, who bestows the gift of "speaking in tongues" on the blessed.

MORMONISM

the 30-second religion

The Church of Jesus Christ of

Latter-day Saints was founded by Joseph Smith in 1830 in Fayette, New York. Mormons believe that Smith received a series of religious visions in which he was given specific instructions and authority to restore the Christian Church. Central to these was the unearthing and translation of a holy book written on plates of gold and containing the story of God's dealings with the ancient people of the Americas, as compiled by the ancient American prophet Mormon. Mormons use this book alongside the Christian Bible (in the Authorized King James Version) in religious teaching and study. Mormons believe in the continuation of prophecy: living prophets are chosen by God to act as means through which revelations can be communicated. For Mormons, all people can receive inspiration from God, but in practice God uses senior Church officials. For Mormons, Jesus is the first-born son of God and the only perfect human being and they believe that by following his example, they might achieve salvation, or the gift of an eternal life with God. Unlike many Christians, Mormons do not believe in original sin, but assert that each individual sins by choosing to do wrong. Hence salvation, while enabled by God's grace, requires the performance of good actions in imitation of Jesus.

3-SECOND SERMON
The Church of Jesus Christ of Latter-day Saints that aims to restore Christianity with new revelations of God's acts and nature.

3-MINUTE THEOLOGY
In contrast to many Christians, Mormons do not believe that God created the universe out of nothing (*ex nihilo*), but that God—the all-powerful and all-knowing supreme being—created it out of preexisting material, which he ordered into its proper forms. For Mormons, God has a physical body (albeit exalted in heaven), Jesus is the perfect first-born son of God, and the Trinity consists of three distinct beings united in a common purpose.

RELATED RELIGIONS
See also
ORTHODOX JUDAISM
Page 60
EUROPEAN CHRISTIANITIES
Pages 78–97
WORLD CHRISTIANITIES
Pages 98–115

3-SECOND BIOGRAPHIES
BRIGHAM YOUNG
1801–1877
JOSEPH SMITH
1805–1844

30-SECOND TEXT
Russell Re Manning

The Book of Mormon, *as translated by Joseph Smith from golden plates, forms the basis of Mormon doctrine and is considered the most "correct text."*

JEHOVAH'S WITNESSES

the 30-second religion

3-SECOND SERMON
The last days began in 1914, leading to the imminent destruction of the world by God's intervention and the deliverance of those who worship Jehovah.

3-MINUTE THEOLOGY
Evangelism is central to Jehovah's Witnesses, in particular, the practice of spreading their beliefs by visiting people's homes. The *Watchtower* commentaries and other teaching material are widely available, with some texts translated into over 500 different languages. Jehovah's Witnesses use and distribute a new translation of the Bible, the *New World Translation of the Holy Scriptures*, of which over 165 million copies have been published in over 80 languages.

The Jehovah's Witnesses is the largest and best known of a group of millenarian restorationist Christian denominations that emerged out of the Bible Student Movement of the late 19th century, founded by Charles Taze Russell. Through continuous preaching and the journal *Zion's Watch Tower and Herald of Christ's Presence*, Russell critiqued many of the established Christian doctrines and taught the urgent message that the second coming of Christ was at hand. Through a mixture of literal and symbolic interpretations of the Bible, Jehovah's Witnesses believe in Russell's predications of the imminent apocalypse—including a cosmic battle between the forces of heaven and the forces of Satan—and the Rapture (assumption into heaven) of all true believers. Jehovah's Witnesses interpret political events, as well as the evidence of global climate change, as proof that the world is coming to an end. Unlike many Christians, Jehovah's Witnesses do not believe in the Holy Trinity, believing God (or "Jehovah" after God's original Biblical name, the Tetragrammaton JHVH, or YHWH) to be Universal Sovereign, Jesus to be God's only direct creation, and the Holy Spirit to be God's power in the world. Jehovah's Witnesses also believe Satan to be a fallen angel, who, along with his demons, misleads people and causes evil and human suffering.

RELATED RELIGIONS
See also
ORTHODOX JUDAISM
Page 60

EUROPEAN CHRISTIANITIES
Pages 78–97

WORLD CHRISTIANITIES
Pages 98–115

3-SECOND BIOGRAPHIES
JESUS
C.5 BCE–C.30 CE

CHARLES TAZE RUSSELL
1852–1916

30-SECOND TEXT
Russell Re Manning

Jehovah's Witnesses believe Russell's prediction that Armageddon will cleanse the earth, and God will create a paradise that will be ruled over by Jesus Christ and 144,000 of the anointed.

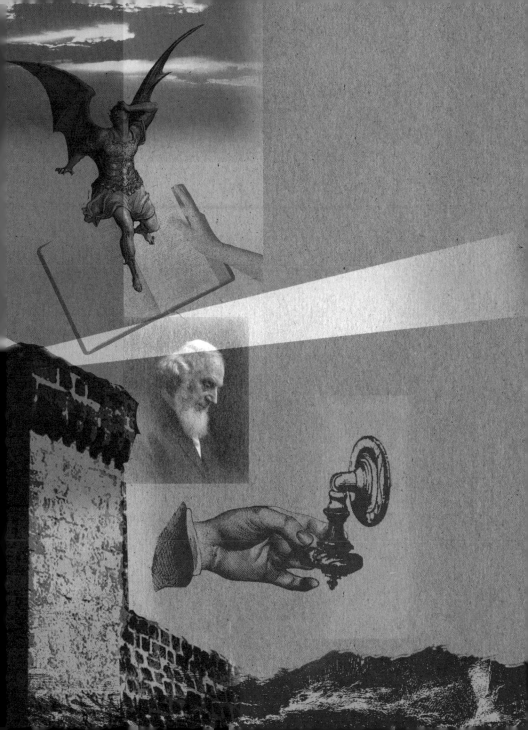

BAPTIST CHRISTIANITY

the 30-second religion

A diverse group of Christian denominations, Baptists take their name from their practice of adult baptism. Unlike most Christians, who baptize infants or young children into the fellowship of the community of Christians (known as "infant baptism, or pedobaptism"), Baptists insist that individual believers freely and publically commit themselves to their Christian faith in a ceremony of adult baptism (known as "believers' baptism," or "credobaptism"). Often these baptisms are full immersions, in which the believer is lowered completely beneath the surface of the water, emerging in the eyes of the Church as "born again" in Christ. Baptist churches emerged in the early 17th century within various Protestant denominations, and, while today there is still no central Baptist authority, two prominent confederations are the Baptist World Alliance (BWA) and the Southern Baptist Convention (SBC). In 2004, the SBC, the largest Protestant denomination in the United States with over 16 million members, voted to leave the BWA over fears of a drift toward theological liberalism. Generally evangelical, Baptists require that the New Testament be the explicit authority for their beliefs and practices. While not always taking the Bible literally, Baptists insist that Christian beliefs and practices are commanded or commended by example within the Bible.

3-SECOND SERMON
Baptism of adult believers is an outward sign of repentance of sins and confession of faith in Jesus Christ as the Son of God.

3-MINUTE THEOLOGY
Baptists believe that religious faith is a matter of a personal relation between God and the believer. This support for "religious freedom" entails that individuals may practice any religion, or none. Historically, they have been ardent supporters of the principle of the separation of Church and State, particularly in the United States. Of course, Baptists have the evangelical hope that individuals will confess a Christian faith, but insist that this must be a free decision.

RELATED RELIGIONS
See also
ORTHODOX JUDAISM
Page 60
EUROPEAN CHRISTIANITIES
Pages 78–97
WORLD CHRISTIANITIES
Pages 98–115

3-SECOND BIOGRAPHIES
JESUS
c.5 BCE–c.30 CE
JOHN SMYTH
c.1570–c.1612
THOMAS HELWYS
c.1575–c.1616
ROGER WILLIAMS
c.1603–1683

30-SECOND TEXT
Russell Re Manning

For Baptists, only adults can profess to a true faith in Jesus Christ and repent of their sins.

SEVENTH-DAY ADVENTIST CHURCH

the 30-second religion

3-SECOND SERMON
A Christian community that observes the Sabbath on Saturday and which is preparing for the imminent return of Jesus Christ.

3-MINUTE THEOLOGY
Seventh-day Adventists believe in so-called "investigative judgment." This is generally meant as an interpretation of Daniel 7:10 and Revelation 20:12, which talk of the opening of the "book of life," in which all the deeds of humanity are written. According to these visions, Satan accuses believers of transgression and unbelief and Jesus acts as advocate, whose atoning sacrifice helps to blot out believers' sins. Those whose names remain are punished by permanent destruction.

Formally established in 1863, the Seventh-day Adventist Church is the largest and most significant Christian Church to have emerged from the Adventist movement of the 1840s, when the imminent "Second Advent" of Jesus Christ was predicted. When this did not happen (known as "the Great Disappointment"), the predictions were reinterpreted to suggest that Christ had entered "the Most Holy Place" of the heavenly sanctuary and that the process of divine judgment had begun. Seventh-day Adventists also believe that the Bible commands Christians to observe the "Sabbath"—that is to keep Saturday (not Sunday) as a day of rest and worship. No secular work may be performed; instead, the day consists of worship, charitable work, and family orientated activities, such as nature walks. Even secular recreational activities, such as competitive sports, are generally avoided. Influenced by the writings of Ellen G. White, Seventh-day Adventists place considerable emphasis on Christian deportment, ranging from sexual ethics of abstinence and strict dietary observance to conservative attitudes toward dress and leisure activities. Although it may not appeal to some, the sober Adventist lifestyle seems to be good for the health: a recent study claims that male Adventist Californians live 7.3 years longer than their non-Adventist neighbors!

RELATED RELIGIONS
See also
EUROPEAN CHRISTIANITIES
Pages 78–97
WORLD CHRISTIANITIES
Pages 98–115

3-SECOND BIOGRAPHIES
JESUS
c.5 BCE–c.30 CE

WILLIAM MILLER
1782–1849

ELLEN G. WHITE
1827–1915

JOHN HARVEY KELLOGG
1852–1943

30-SECOND TEXT
Russell Re Manning

A healthy body and a healthy soul—Adventists emphasize health through abstinence from alcohol, tobacco, and often meat.

CHRISTIAN SCIENCE

the 30-second religion

In 1875, Mary Baker Eddy

published a book entitled *Science and Health with Key to the Scriptures*. Eddy, who had been experiencing persistent health problems for many years, tells of how in 1866 she had recovered unexpectedly from a bad fall and had founded the new religion of Christian Science. In 1879, the First Church of Christ, Scientist was founded in Boston, Massachusetts. Central to Christian Science is the belief that prayer can lead to healing and, in most cases, should be preferred to conventional medical treatment. This is not, however, because God is thought to intervene miraculously in the world. Instead, Christian Scientists believe the material world to be a distorted version of the true world—a world of spiritual ideas. Prayer enables an undistorted vision of the spiritual reality. Illness is understood to be the result of a mistaken conviction in the reality of a material problem; hence, healing is the removal of this error by the recognition that the problem is only really an illusion. Christian Scientists regard Jesus Christ as the "Wayshower" and consider his healing "miracles" as exemplars of his spiritual understanding: an understanding that is available to all humanity.

3-SECOND SERMON
The real world is an immortal reality of spiritual ideas; recognize this and healing follows.

3-MINUTE THEOLOGY
For Christian Scientists, the relation between Christian belief and the natural sciences is simple. The natural sciences describe the unreal world of the material and as such are illusory; instead Christian Science leads to an understanding of the real immortal world of spiritual ideas. There is no real conflict: the natural scientific accounts of biological evolution are as mistaken as "Creationist" accounts: both come from the belief in the reality of the material world.

RELATED RELIGIONS
See also
EUROPEAN CHRISTIANITIES
Pages 78–97
WORLD CHRISTIANITIES
Pages 98–115

3-SECOND BIOGRAPHIES
JESUS
C.5 BCE–C.30 CE

MARY BAKER EDDY
1821–1910

30-SECOND TEXT
Russell Re Manning

God encompasses the spiritual reality, which is truth and good. According to Christian Scientists, the material world, including evil, is unreal and false.

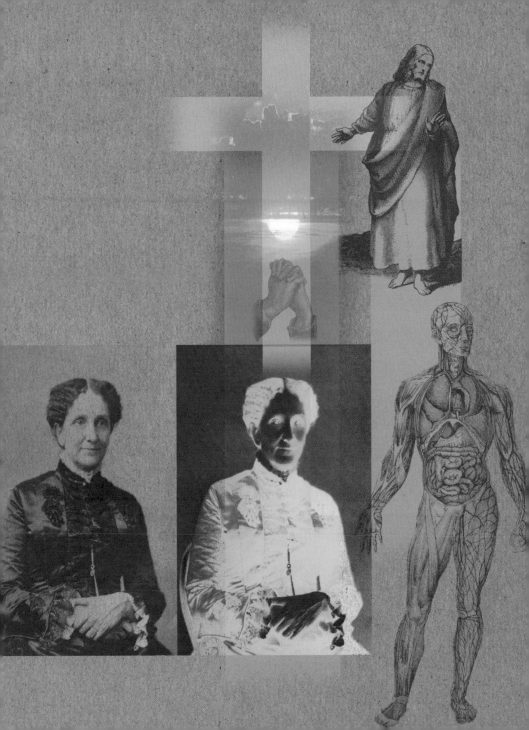

FUSION RELIGIONS

animal sacrifice The ritual killing of an animal to appease or petition deities. It is sometimes interpreted as the killing of humankind's baser, "animal" instincts, or simply as sacrificing something precious to prove devotion. Many religions practice animal sacrifice, including Hinduism, and there are numerous descriptions of it in the Old Testament.

Bhagavad Gita A section of the Mahabharata, composed in c.250 BCE, in which Krishna reveals himself to Arjuna and embarks on a long theological discussion about human nature and the meaning of life. Many of the central tenets of Hinduism are discussed, including the dissolution of ego and following the natural path.

black magic The channeling of malevolent spirits and other paranormal phenomena to create spells and bring about evil deeds, or the belief that this is possible.

Christian spiritualists People who combine their Christian faith with spiritualist beliefs. The main attraction for such people is the alleged ability to contact the dead and communicate with their loved ones. Orthodox Christian religions maintain that the Bible expressly forbids contacts with the dead, quoting passages from Deuteronomy (18:11) and Luke (16:19–31).

ectoplasm A substance said to exude from various orifices, or possibly the pores, of mediums while they are in a trance. Starting as a smoke or vapor, it is said to react to light and turn into a clothlike substance.

medium A person who is said to contact the spirits of the dead and other paranormal forces and to act as an intermediary with the living. Contact is usually made when the medium falls into a trance and allows the spirit to use his or her body to communicate either verbally or through writing or other signs. The practice is prevalent in certain religions, such as Spiritualism and Voodooism.

Odin In Norse mythology, the supreme God, who created heaven, earth, and the first human beings, Ask and Embla. He was also venerated as the god of poetry, wisdom, knowledge, magic, prophecy, war, hunting, victory, and death.

pantheon A temple devoted to the gods, such as the building of that name in Rome, or a collective name for a group of gods or deities.

paranormal Something that cannot be explained by normal experience or currently accepted scientific laws. Typical examples are telepathy, divination, astrology, channeling, ghosts, and UFOs.

Satanists Those who worship Satan. The term is sometimes used by Christian fundamentalists to describe all non-Christians. The real Church of Satan, however, has well-defined principles, such as fulfilling desires and not turning the other cheek, but also being kind to those who deserve it and not harming children.

séance A meeting of people, usually around a table, to contact the spirits of the dead. A medium is usually used as an intermediary, and messages are relayed in the form of speech, writing, cards, or Ouija boards. From the French meaning "to be seated," originally it referred to any meeting but especially meetings of the legislature.

shamanism The belief that the world is filled with spirits, which can be influenced by a holy man. The shaman is thought to be able to heal people and resolve problems within communities by connecting with the spirit world and restoring balance. The religion is prevalent in Asia and Siberia and among Native American tribes.

spirit The nonphysical, metaphysical part of a person; their essential life force. Many religions consider that it is the spirit that gives the body life, and that the spirit survives after the body has died.

syncretism The merging of different faiths, usually implying a successful new fusion. Christian Spiritualism is one example. The Baha'i faith, which accepts Muhammad, Jesus, Moses, Buddha, Zoroaster, and Abraham as prophets, is considered another, although it has its own prophet, Bahá'u'lláh, and its own holy scriptures.

Wicca A pagan or nature-based religion that is said to have its roots in pre-Christian witchcraft. Covens of Wiccans use magic rituals to celebrate seasonal festivals based around a Mother Goddess. Some claim sexual acts are involved.

zombie A dead body brought to life by supernatural forces. In Voodoo religions, the term can also refer to a spell cast to bring a corpse back to life and control it. The concept originates in West Africa but has been popularized in Western popular culture through novels and movies.

NEO-PAGANISM

the 30-second religion

Neo-Pagans are inspired by the

ancient pre-Christian religions of Europe (and, to a lesser extent, the Middle East), and there is a diversity of beliefs and emphases. Hellenic Neo-Pagans, for example, worship Greek deities, such as Zeus, while others look to Norse gods, such as Odin. The best-known strand, however, is known as Wicca, which stresses the notion of a Goddess of fertility and rebirth, and her male consort, the Horned God of the forests. Nature is to be respected and celebrated—both in the rhythm of the year and the life cycle—and humans in harmony with nature can become adepts of "the Craft," the use of magic. However, such self-described "witches" are cautioned to use magic for healing and for personal development instead of for outward manipulation. Some Neo-Pagans regard the deities as real beings, others as symbolic representations of natural forces and aspects of human characteristics. Much of the scholarship on "the Goddess" that Wicca draws on is today regarded as historically problematic, but members are often aware of this and are willing to regard such texts as "founding myths."

RELATED RELIGION
See also
ANIMISM
Page 18

3-SECOND BIOGRAPHIES
GERALD GARDNER
1884–1964

ALEX SANDERS
1926–1988

MAXINE SANDERS
1946–

STARHAWK
1951–

30-SECOND TEXT
Richard Bartholomew

3-SECOND SERMON
Humans should live in harmony with nature by venerating ancient gods and goddesses, while magical rituals can bring healing and spiritual growth.

3-MINUTE THEOLOGY
With its stress on a female divinity and its empowering reclamation of the label "witch," Wicca in particular has attracted some feminist support. However, because the Goddess is often portrayed as a stereotypically alluring, slim young woman, the movement has been critiqued for entrenching gender essentialism. Neo-Pagan practices—particularly those that involve nudity—are regarded with hostility by many Christians, and Wiccans have often complained of being accused of Satanism by churches and the media.

Neo-Paganism is an essentially polytheistic, religion, recognizing a divine Goddess, and celebrating nature as a divinity in its own right.

SPIRITUALISM

the 30-second religion

Spiritualists believe that mediums can convey messages from the spirit world. Communications may be religious teachings from a spirit guide, or personal messages from deceased loved ones. A spirit may communicate in various ways: the medium may go into a trance and either speak the spirit's words or write them down—if the medium is consulted during a séance, in which a small group of people sit around a table, the spirit may answer by rapping on the table or by tipping it. Alternatively, the medium may stand before a larger audience and claim to receive personal information from a variety of spirits about particular people present. Some mediums advertise themselves as able to provide messages for people who contact them by telephone or text message; in the past, some claimed that during their trance their bodies would exude ectoplasm, a substance that would form into the image of the spirit and which could be photographed. Despite the Biblical taboo against contacting the dead, there are Christian Spiritualists, some of whom emphasize teachings received from a disciple of Jesus called Zodiac. The spirit world is thought to consist of various levels or "spheres"; spiritual progression continues after death.

3-SECOND SERMON
The dead can communicate from the spirit world with the living via mediums, providing information and other manifestations that scientifically prove life after death.

3-MINUTE THEOLOGY
Spiritualism claims to offer scientific evidence for the afterlife, in the form of information that the medium could not have known without communication with spirits. As such, it has attracted considerable interest from investigators of paranormal phenomena, some of whom have become convinced that mediumship is genuine. Others, however, believe that, due to wishful thinking, those who consult mediums overlook incorrect information and the medium's ability to coax or discern information naturally.

3-SECOND BIOGRAPHIES
EMANUEL SWEDENBORG
1688–1772

MARGARET FOX
1833–1893

LEONORA PIPER
1857–1950

ARTHUR CONAN DOYLE
1859–1930

DORIS STOKES
1920–1987

30-SECOND TEXT
Richard Bartholomew

Spiritualists believe that the spirit survives death. Messages from the spirit world are relayed to the living via mediums.

VOODOO

the 30-second religion

According to the beliefs of

Voodoo, there are thousands of spirits (*lwa*) that interact with humanity. These *lwa* were once human, and they are classified into "nations" that reflect the ancestral homelands of African slaves. Some spirits are generous *rada* spirits, while others are more aggressive *petro* spirits, although these can be seen as alternative manifestations of the same *lwa*. Certain spirits are particularly associated with the dead; these are the *gede*, headed by Baron Samdi and known for their trickery and raucous behavior. The spirits were all created by the Supreme God, Bondye, who considers petitions from humans conveyed by the *lwa* but who is otherwise uninvolved with humanity. The *lwa* are served by Voodoo priests (*oungan*) and priestesses (*manbo*), and contact with the *lwa* can occur through dreams, possession trances, or divination. Rituals include drumming and dancing, because these attract the spirits and induce possession, while animal sacrifice provides the spirits with sustenance. There are also malign lesser spirits, *baka*, who can be manipulated for selfish purposes by sorcerers, called *boko*. *Boko* are also thought to have the power to create zombies; these are bodies controlled by the *boko* by capture of the owner's soul.

RELATED RELIGIONS
See also
YORUBA
Page 14
CANDOMBLÉ
Page 126

3-SECOND BIOGRAPHIES
BOUKMAN DUTTY
d. c.1791

MARIE LAVEAU
1794–1881

MAYA DEREN
1917–1961

30-SECOND TEXT
Richard Bartholomew

3-SECOND SERMON
Many spirits make themselves known through dreams, trances, and communication with priests; Voodoo rituals provide healing, assistance, and protection from evil forces.

3-MINUTE THEOLOGY
Many followers of Voodoo consider themselves to be Roman Catholics, despite the Church's antagonistic attitude toward the religion. Many of the *lwa* are identified with Roman Catholic saints—such is the gatekeeper *lwa* Legba; he is often associated with Saint Peter, who in Catholic tradition holds the keys to heaven. Some Voodoo practitioners complain about the lurid way in which the religion is depicted in popular culture as a form of "black magic."

Intoxicating rituals open contact with the spirit world, allowing Voodoo priests and priestesses to seek assistance and healing.

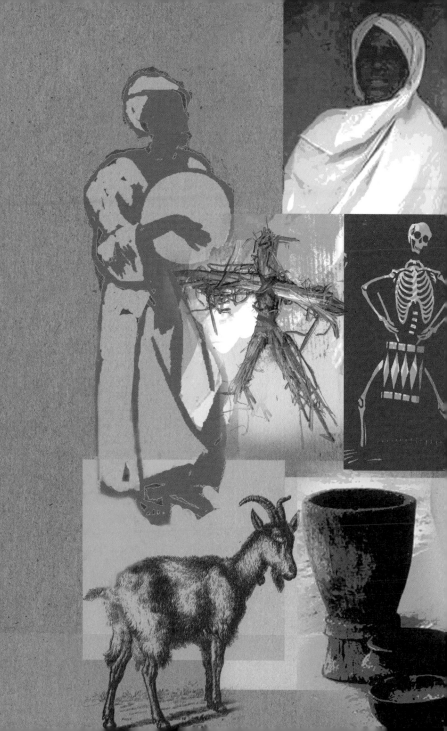

CANDOMBLÉ

the 30-second religion

Followers of Candomblé venerate

African deities, drawing on traditions from several parts of Africa (but primarily Yoruba) that were brought to Brazil by slaves. The deities are known as *orixás*, although there is some variation of nomenclature; there is a distant high God named Olorun, his son Oxalá, who created the world, and a small pantheon of other deities representing aspects of human experience and the natural order, such as war and agriculture (Ogum) and luxury and fertility (Oxum). Each person is the "child" of a particular *orixá*, and a follower of the religion (either a woman or a man) may choose to become an *iaô*, an initiate of a deity. Following the initiation process, the *iaô* represents the deity to the people, entering trance possessions and dancing, and after seven years the *iaô* may become a *mãe* or *pie de santo* (mother or father of saints). The gods are offered animal sacrifices, and they are consulted about problems through divination methods, such as throwing down cowry shells and interpreting the resulting pattern. Health and harmony depend on achieving a balance between the various forces represented by the different *orixás*.

RELATED RELIGIONS
See also
YORUBA
Page 14
VOODOO
Page 124

3-SECOND SERMON
The gods give us life, protection, and advice, so we should reciprocate with food offerings, celebrations, and, in some cases, initiations.

3-MINUTE THEOLOGY
Candomblé has traditionally contained elements taken from Roman Catholicism, with the *orixás* identified with Jesus and the saints. Followers of Candomblé also typically describe themselves as Roman Catholics. However, since the 1980s there has been a movement to reject Catholic influence as a "syncretistic" imposition; those who take this view seek "re-Africanization" and advise the removal of Catholic images. However, some scholars believe that this quest for purity belies the historical complexities in the development of Candomblé.

3-SECOND BIOGRAPHIES
IYA NASSO
fl.1830s

MÃE ANINHA
Eugênia Anna Santos
1879–1938

MÃE MENININHA
Maria Escolástica
da Conceição Nazaré
1894–1986

MÃE STELLA DE OXOSSI
Maria Stella
de Azevedo Santos
1925–

30-SECOND TEXT
Richard Bartholomew

With strong African associations, Candomblé followers look to the gods for security in return for offerings and veneration.

HARE KRISHNA MOVEMENT

the 30-second religion

RELATED RELIGION
See also
HINDUISM
Page 32

3-SECOND BIOGRAPHIES
A. C. BHAKTIVEDANTA
SWAMI PRABHUPADA
1896–1977

GEORGE HARRISON
1943–2001

RAVINDRA SVARUPA DASA
William H. Deadwyler
c.1946

30-SECOND TEXT
Richard Bartholomew

3-SECOND SERMON
Sincere devotion to Krishna expressed through chanting, service, and right living will lead to God consciousness.

3-MINUTE THEOLOGY
Despite its conservative moral strictures and patriarchy, ISKCON's first appeal was to members of the 1960s counterculture, most famously George Harrison. However, following the death of Prabhupada, the organization experienced scandals involving gurus who were expelled for engaging in illicit sex and using drugs. While Prabhupada regarded the religion in universal terms, ISKCON today places greater stress on its Hindu background, and non-ISKCON Hindus are known to attend ISKCON temples for worship.

The International Society for Krishna Consciousness (ISKCON) believes that the Hindu deity Krishna represents the supreme manifestation of God, and that he has been incarnated at various times in history, including as Rama and The Buddha. Most recently, he came as Chaitanya Mahaprabhu (1486–1533), who taught salvation through devotion (*bhakti*). ISKCON members express their love for Krishna by worship practices that include public dancing and preaching, and by repeating a 16-word mantra taken from the Hindu *Upanishads*, and which begins "Hare Krishna" ("Hare" refers to the energy of God). Through such activities the law of karma and the cycle of reincarnation will be overcome, although the ordinary devotee must remain under the guidance of a recognized guru within the movement, and moral precepts must be followed. The words of Krishna are believed to be recorded in the Bhagavad Gita, and adherents consider that the purest translation into English and most authoritative commentary was made by A. C. Bhaktivedanta Swami Prabhupada, who founded ISKCON in the United States in 1966. ISKCON is noted for providing free meals, both as a charitable act for the needy and to promote the virtues of vegetarianism, and for its mass distribution of literature.

Adherents of the Hare Krishna movement worship Krishna as the Supreme Lord and aim to promote spirituality, peace, and unity.

CHEONDOISM

the 30-second religion

Adherents believe that the Ruler

of Heaven, Sangje, revealed himself to a young Korean scholar named Ch'oe Che'u in 1860. Sangje gave Ch'oe Che'u a cryptic phrase, which, when written on paper and swallowed, will cure disease and impart long life. Repeating the phrase in worship is believed to help humans to bring their thoughts and actions into harmony with heaven. In addition, humans should work to build a paradise on earth, and this has been understood to mean support for Korean nationalism. The teaching is characterized as "Eastern Learning" (*Tonghak*, the original name of the religion), in conscious opposition to "Western Learning" (*Sohak*), which was identified with Roman Catholicism. However, although the name "Sangje" comes from Chinese Taoism, the religion has a central prayer which uses the Roman Catholic term for God, "Chonju," and worship style and architecture suggest influence from Protestantism. The current name of the religion, adopted in 1905, means "Religion of the Heavenly Way."

3-SECOND SERMON
Humans and heaven are one, and humans can realize this truth by reverencing the Ruler of Heaven and repeating a sacred phrase.

3-MINUTE THEOLOGY
Cheondoism blends Chinese religion with Korean shamanism in the context of a nationalistic Korean identity. Ch'oe Che'u was executed for treason in 1864, and leaders of the group led insurrections against corrupt rulers in the 1890s. A later leader, Son Pyong-hui, helped to write the Korean Declaration of Independence, and in the 1960s members were prominent in patriotic pro-government rallies in South Korea.

RELATED RELIGIONS
See also
ANIMISM
Page 18

MAINSTREAM BUDDHISM
Page 36

TAOISM
Page 48

3-SECOND BIOGRAPHIES
CH'OE CHE'U
1824–1864

CH'OE SIHYONG
1827–1898

SON PYONG-HUI
1861–1922

30-SECOND TEXT
Richard Bartholomew

The repetition of a sacred phrase provided by the Ruler of Heaven will bring about harmony between heaven and earth.

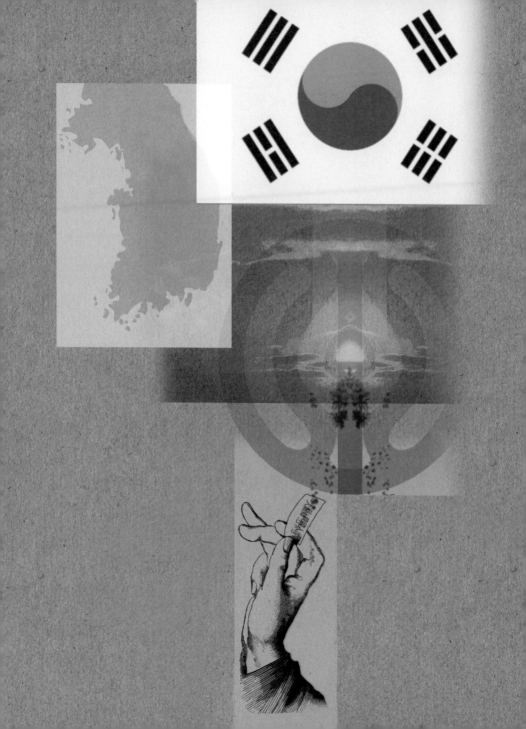

TENRIKYO

the 30-second religion

Followers of Tenrikyo believe

that from 1838 God the Parent (Tenri-O-no-mikoto) began to reveal himself through Nakayama Miki, a farmer's wife who was declared to be the Shrine of God and "Oyasama," meaning "Parent." God the Parent conveyed through Oyasama the promise that, following rebirths, humans will eventually experience an age in which everyone will enjoy the "joyous life;" suffering is due to causation (*innen*, or karmic fate). The path to the "joyous life" is to express gratitude for the life loaned to us by God, to understand that all people are brothers and sisters, and to detach ourselves from negative "dusts," such as envy or hate that settle in our minds and cause selfishness. Oyasama embodied the path by giving away her family's wealth and impoverishing herself. God the Parent later revealed that a location within the historical heartland of Japan is the center of the universe; this place, now within the city of Tenri in Nara, is where God the Parent resides, and it was here that humanity was created. Today, it is a place of pilgrimage, and it is venerated with sacred dance. Oyasama's male descendants now lead the religion.

RELATED RELIGIONS
See also
MAHAYANA BUDDHISM
Page 40
SHINTO
Page 54
SHINSHUKYO
Page 150

3-SECOND BIOGRAPHIES
NAKAYAMA MIKI
1798–1887

IBURI IZO
1833–1907

30-SECOND TEXT
Richard Bartholomew

3-SECOND SERMON
God the Parent wants all humans to partake of the "joyous life" through moral cultivation.

3-MINUTE THEOLOGY
Tenrikyo draws on folk shamanism and Buddhism, and despite the emphasis on Japan as the center of the universe, the religion regards itself as having a message for the whole world. However, it also shares elements with Shinto, and from 1908 to 1970 it was formally assimilated by the state into a form of Shinto. During her lifetime, Oyasama's message of equality and her female leadership were regarded with suspicion as well as hostility by the Japanese authorities.

Echoing the Buddhist belief in reincarnation, Tenrikyo teaches that attainment of the "joyous life" is achieved by denying negative tendencies.

天理市

NEW RELIGIONS

Babylon The most important city in ancient Mesopotamia, located on the Euphrates River, 50 miles (80 km) south of Baghdad. It was the capital of the Babylonian Empire from 612 BCE. To Rastafarians, Babylon is a symbol of the oppression of blacks by whites, just as the Jews were oppressed during the Persian rule of Babylon in 538–332 BCE.

black supremacy The belief that black people are superior to other races. At its most extreme, it is a racist ideology that encourages hatred toward anyone not of African ancestry, especially whites and Jews. However, some historians suggest that black supremacy is simply a reaction to white racism. Key organizations in the promotion of black supremacy are the Nation of Islam, formed in 1930, and the Black Panther Party, formed in 1966.

divine eye The symbol of the Cao Dai religion; a left-hand eye inside a circle or triangle. The eye is supposed to remind followers that the Supreme Being is "all seeing" and "all knowing" and that their every action is being watched. The left eye is shown because left represents yang, or the holy spirit, which watches over humankind.

dreadlocks Hair that is grown long, is twisted, and then becomes matted into long coils that look like rope. Although also practiced by other religions, dreadlocks are particularly associated with Rastafarians, who wear "dreads" as an expression of religious belief and to assert their black identity. Several passages from the Bible are quoted to support the practice, including Leviticus 21:5 and Numbers 6:5.

livity The Rastafarian way of life. This includes rejecting Babylon, or the modern way of life, by not paying taxes, only eating additive-free food, avoiding alcohol and coffee, smoking cannabis, eating a mainly vegetarian diet—or at very least not eating pork and shellfish—and growing hair into dreadlocks. The Rastafarian ethos has been criticized for its negative attitude to women and homosexuals.

Lucifer The word "Lucifer" is derived from the Latin *lux* (light) and *ferre* (to bear), meaning the light bearer, and original referred to the morning star. The term was used in the New Testament to refer to a Babylonian king who fell from power (Isaiah 14:3–20) and only later was the name applied to the devil. Nowadays, the word is used almost interchangeably with Satan, the devil, and Beelzebub.

Messiah The savior of the Jews, whose arrival is anticipated in the Old Testament. For Christians, Jesus of Nazareth fulfilled the prophecies and became their Messiah. More generally, the term is used to refer to any savior figure. From the Hebrew word *masiah*, meaning "anointed one."

Operating Thetan According to Scientology, the spiritual rank above "Clear." Once humans have been audited, they reach a state of "Clear." After that, further study will enable them to become Operating Thetans. There are many stages thereafter, with OTI-VII being preliminary stages before becoming a fully fledged OT at OTVIII, when the full truth is revealed.

qigong A Chinese martial art that combines meditation and movement. The full technique includes 460 movements, which involve visualizations and breathing exercises. Originating in China in 1122 BCE, the aim is to harmonize mind and body. From the Chinese *qi* or *chi* (energy) and *gong* (cultivation).

reincarnation Similar to the Buddhist concept of rebirth, except it is applied to a specific individual soul, instead of the more general concept of an "evolving consciousness." This idea is central to most Eastern religions, including Hinduism, Jainism, and Sikhism.

Supreme Being God, in the Cao Dai religion. The term is used to avoid any gender, race, or religious associations, although it is explicitly the same god worshipped by all other religions. The aim of the Cao Dai is to unite all believers in a supreme being.

syncretism The merging of different faiths, usually implying a successful new fusion. Christian Spiritualism is one example. The Baha'i Faith, which accepts Muhammad, Jesus, Moses, Buddha, Zoroaster, and Abraham as prophets, is considered another, although it has its own prophet, Bahá'u'lláh, and its own holy scriptures.

Thetan According to Scientology, the essence of life, similar to the soul in other religions. Thetans were self-willed into existence trillions of years ago and created the physical world for their own amusement. However, in time they forgot their true nature and became locked in their physical bodies. The aim of Scientology is to return them to their original state of "self-determinism."

Zion Originally a hill in Jerusalem conquered by David, but also a general term for a promised land. For Rastafarians, Zion is located in Ethiopia.

JOHN FRUM MOVEMENT

the 30-second religion

Believers regard John Frum as

God; he is thought to divide his time between America and Yasur, a volcano on the island of Tanna in Vanuatu, in the South Pacific. He first made himself known to local inhabitants in the 1930s through a vision, urging the rejection of Christianity and colonial currency, and a return to *kastom*—traditional culture. These were the customs and traditions that missionaries had forbidden, such as drinking an intoxicant called *kava*. Followers believe that subsequent events vindicated their faith: World War II brought sailors dressed in white to the island, along with technological marvels. Although these Americans left after the war, John Frum will one day return with a bounty of cargo from the United States. Believers offer prayers to Frum, and each year celebrate John Frum Day; ceremonies include raising U.S. flags and marching in mock U.S. uniforms, and replica chain saws are swung symbolically to prepare space for the building of factories. Members of the movement have also constructed an airstrip with bamboo control towers to facilitate the arrival of the cargo.

3-SECOND SERMON
John Frum is King of America, and he will make the island of Tanna into a utopia by restoring traditional customs and bringing cargo.

3-MINUTE THEOLOGY
The John Frum Movement is categorized as a "cargo cult." However, followers are not just motivated by a desire for material goods: the movement began as a protest against colonial domination. The movement's relationship with authorities in Vanuatu is tense. Paradoxically, it defends *kastom* by appropriating symbols of technology and of the United States, and it rejects Christianity while adapting millenarian Christian beliefs about a coming New World.

3-SECOND BIOGRAPHIES
NAMBAS
fl.1950s

NAKOMAHA
fl.1950s

ISAAK WAN
Current

FRED NESSE
Current

30-SECOND TEXT
Richard Bartholomew

Followers believe that John Frum, King of America, will return, bringing wealth and the reestablishment of traditional customs.

FALUN GONG

the 30-second religion

Falun Gong is based on the

teachings of Li Hongzhi, a former musician who is regarded by followers as a master of qigong, a form of Chinese meditation and exercise used for healing and for increasing human potential. Li draws on popular Buddhism and Taoism, and he relates health to karma, in which actions in one's past lives affect one's current life. Karma is a black substance inside the body, which, through suffering or practice alongside moral living, can be made white. Followers should read Li's writings, get rid of "attachments," and follow the exercises that he prescribes; practitioners may develop paranormal powers, and Li claims to have a greater understanding of the universe than can be known by science. This includes the knowledge that aliens exist, and that the world has been destroyed and recreated a number of times and is about to undergo this process again. A sign that this is about to occur is the repression that followers have experienced in China since 1999; Li says that those who suffer or die for their belief will receive instant enlightenment. Members have held silent protests in Beijing and outside Chinese embassies abroad.

3-SECOND SERMON
Certain exercises will transform the body and reveal a person's place in the universe; a new world cycle of destruction and renewal is imminent.

3-MINUTE THEOLOGY
In the People's Republic of China, Falun Gong is regarded as a "heretical cult" that exploits members, causes deaths, and is a threat to society. Practitioners have been detained and sent to labor camps, although claims of organ harvesting reported in Falun Gong media, such as the *Epoch Times*, are unsubstantiated. In 2001, Li was awarded a prize by Freedom House, a prominent American human rights organization, as a "defender of religious rights."

RELATED RELIGIONS
See also
MAINSTREAM BUDDHISM
Page 36
TAOISM
Page 48

3-SECOND BIOGRAPHY
LI HONGZHI
1952–

30-SECOND TEXT
Richard Bartholomew

Adherents of Falun Gong seek enlightenment through the practice of qigong and the teachings of Li Hongzhi.

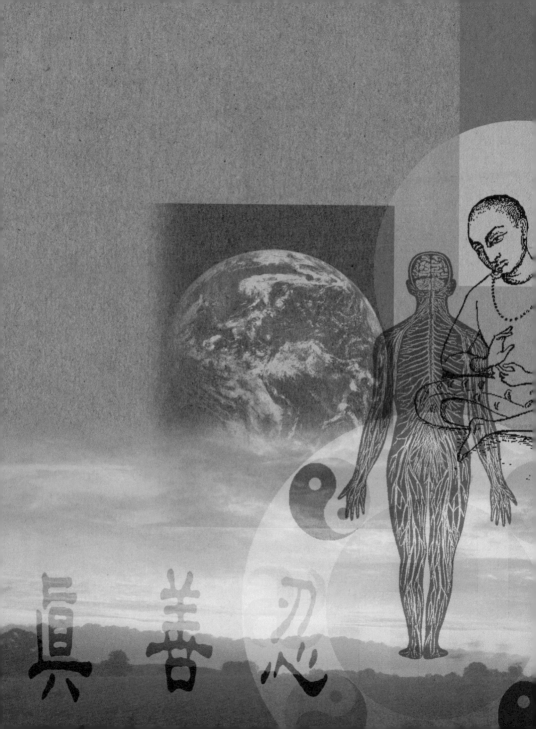

UNIFICATION CHURCH

the 30-second religion

RELATED RELIGIONS
See also
CONFUCIANISM
Page 50
CALVINISM
Page 90

3-SECOND SERMON
The perfect marriage of the Messiah restores humanity's bond with God; Rev. Moon is the "True Father" who completes the work of Jesus.

3-MINUTE THEOLOGY
Although the theology of the Unification Church diverges from traditional Christianity, Moon was raised as a Presbyterian and he regards his theology as Christian. Organizations founded by the church promote interfaith activities and Moon's emphasis on marriage has attracted some African Catholic clerics whose own church demands that priests be celibate. Moon's parents had formerly been Confucians before they became Christians, and the scholar Ninian Smart described Moon's teachings as "Evangelical Confucianism."

Unificationists believe that God's plan is for his love to be made manifest through a perfect trinity of God, man, and woman, expressed through the "ideal family." However, the bond between humans and God was broken when Eve, the first woman, had intercourse with the angel Lucifer, and then with the first man. Jesus came to restore the trinity by having a family, but he was crucified before he could complete his work. Sun Myung Moon (born in Korea in 1920) claims to be the Messiah come again as the "True Father," while his wife is the "True Mother." Adherents believe that their bond with God is restored through taking part in a mass wedding ceremony performed by Moon, with a partner chosen by the Church. As a sign that humanity is one family, many Unificationist couples are international or interracial and Moon teaches that their children will be without the Original Sin inherited from Adam and Eve. Moon warns that the human sexual organs are precious and must be used properly; "free love" and homosexuality should disappear. Such teachings are called the "Divine Principle." Moon does not believe he is God and believers object to being called "Moonies."

3-SECOND BIOGRAPHIES
SUN MYUNG MOON
"True Father"
1920–

HAK JA HAN MOON
"True Mother"
1943–

HYO JIN MOON
1962–2008

HYUN JIN (PRESTON) MOON
1969–

30-SECOND TEXT
Richard Bartholomew

Mass wedding ceremonies symbolize the reunification between God, man, and woman—the perfect trinity.

CAO DAI

the 30-second religion

Cao Dai was established in southern Vietnam in 1926. It teaches that the religious founders and other great figures of the past represent two earlier eras of divine communication with the world. The Third Era was revealed to a Vietnamese civil servant named Ngo Minh Chieu, when he was contacted by a spirit named Cao Dai during a séance; the name means "Roofless Tower," and refers to the "Supreme Being." Believers also adhere to further teachings delivered through mediums, both directly from Cao Dai and through various disembodied spirits of the dead. One such spirit is that of the French author Victor Hugo, who is thought to have been the Supreme Being's messenger to the West. Clergy are divided into three subgroups representing Buddhism, Confucianism, and Taoism, and organized along a structure borrowed from Roman Catholicism (although there is no Pope at present, and women are allowed some positions). The Supreme Being is symbolized as a left eye, called the Celestial Eye, and significant figures such as The Buddha and Jesus are among a group of deities at levels below Cao Dai. Adherents believe in karma, and seek merit through religious practice and service to society to escape the cycle of reincarnation.

3-SECOND SERMON
This is the Third Era of Salvation; religions are united in the worship of the Supreme Being, and there is communication with the spirit world.

3-MINUTE THEOLOGY
Cao Dai represents a modernizing synthesis that began by appealing to educated Vietnamese living under colonial rule; this modern perspective includes the emphasis on spirit contact, since Western spiritualist phenomena have been regarded in some circles as scientific. Cao Dai is also associated with anticolonialism, and festivals and exhibitions organized by the religion have celebrated progress and spiritual evolution by showing members in modern professions.

RELATED RELIGIONS
See also
MAINSTREAM BUDDHISM
Page 36
TAOISM
Page 48
CONFUCIANISM
Page 50
SPIRITUALISM
Page 122

3-SECOND BIOGRAPHIES
LE VAN TRUNG
1875–1934

NGO MINH CHIEU
1878–1932

PHAM CONG TAC
1890–1959

30-SECOND TEXT
Richard Bartholomew

Utilizing elements of Buddhism, Cao Dai, through the teachings of the eponymous Supreme Being, will lead followers to break the cycle of reincarnation.

SCIENTOLOGY

the 30-second religion

According to L. Ron Hubbard's

book *Dianetics* (1950), humans are limited by "engrams," bad experiences stored in the unconscious mind that affect behavior. These experiences may be from earlier in one's life, from the womb, or from past lives. Engrams can be removed through a process called "auditing"—this involves answering questions, either using the book or in a professional environment while attached to a device invented by Hubbard called the E-Meter. Psychiatry, by contrast, is rejected as harmful, particularly in its use of drugs. Those who have completed the process are called "Clears." Hubbard's subsequent teaching states that a "Clear" can further develop the inner self, called a "Thetan." A Scientologist seeks to become an Operating Thetan (OT), and then to pass through various levels. At OT III, a Scientologist learns about how the Thetans were brought to the earth by Xenu, a galactic dictator, in traumatic circumstances 75 million years ago. However, this knowledge is believed to be dangerous to the unprepared, and it will be meaningful only if revealed in a ritual context. Hubbard discovered this through scientific investigation, not through revelation, although some Scientologists regard the story as allegorical. Hubbard is venerated as the greatest author, inventor, and explorer.

3-SECOND SERMON
Human functioning and awareness can be dramatically improved, and with progress comes personal development from secret knowledge about the history of the universe.

3-MINUTE THEOLOGY
Hubbard is reported to have said in the 1940s that he would like to start a religion to make money, and skeptics allege that Scientology is not a real religion. The Church is known for having an aggressive attitude to critics, and in the 1970s it was beset with allegations of criminality in more than one country in pursuit of its interests. Recently, masked anti-Scientologist activists calling themselves "Anonymous" have picketed Scientologist establishments.

3-SECOND BIOGRAPHIES
L. RON HUBBARD
1911–1986

MARY SUE HUBBARD
1932–2002

MICHAEL MISCAVAGE
1960–

30-SECOND TEXT
Richard Bartholomew

Having divested yourself of bad engrams, as a "Clear" you can embark on a series of stages that will reveal the true history of the universe.

RASTAFARIAN MOVEMENT
the 30-second religion

The Rastafarian movement
began in Jamaica, when the coronation of Ras Tafari as Emperor Haile Selassie of Ethiopia in 1930 was interpreted as a prophetic event by some black Jamaicans. While the Caribbean and most of Africa were under white colonial domination, Ethiopia remained a proud and independent black African nation, and Haile Selassie, as God, would restore black supremacy and bring blacks back to Africa. The Bible, complemented by other texts, was interpreted in the light of the situation of blacks: just as the ancient empire of Babylon had oppressed the Jews, so whites were "Babylon" oppressing the black chosen people, considered reincarnated Israelites, and Ethiopia was Zion. Believers express their identity through the "livity," a way of life that emphasizes naturalness. Hair is worn as dreadlocks, diet is vegetarian, and herbal medicine is favored; in particular, ganja (marijuana) is regarded as a sacrament that brings spiritual healing when smoked. Language is adapted to convey Rastafarian experience: human dignity and subjectivity are expressed by using "I" instead of the Creole *mi* (me), and the divine essence inside each person is called "I and I."

3-SECOND SERMON
God redeems black people from white oppression, and he came to the earth as Haile Selassie, the Emperor of Ethiopia.

3-MINUTE THEOLOGY
The figure of Haile Selassie (who died in 1975) is no longer central for many Rastafarians, and the idea of a return to Africa is often understood symbolically in terms of self-expression within white-majority societies. Personal liberation not black supremacy is stressed, and there are now also white Rastafarians. However, despite the emphasis on liberation, the religion remains patriarchal, and Rasta women have complained about their subordinate position within the religion.

3-SECOND BIOGRAPHIES
HAILE SELASSIE
1892–1975

JOSEPH HIBBERT
1894–date unknown

MARCUS GARVEY
1887–1940

LEONARD PERCIVAL HOWELL
1898–1981

ARCHIBALD DUNKLEY
fl.1930s

BOB MARLEY
1945–1981

30-SECOND TEXT
Richard Bartholomew

God, manifest as the Emperor Haile Selassie, arrived on the earth to help raise black consciousness.

SHINSHUKYO

the 30-second religion

Japanese religion is characterized
by syncretism and decentralization: typically,
a birth is marked by a Shinto ceremony and
Buddhism provides funeral services. "Shinshukyo"
refers to "Newly Rising Religions," although in
fact many groups so described draw on various
aspects of this diverse and ancient religious
heritage as interpreted by a particular individual.
These founders and religious leaders, for
adherents, make religion relevant for today,
and the organizations that promote their
teachings have replaced older patterns of
religious affiliation. Some leaders, following the
shamanistic aspects of Japanese religion, are
believed to be channeling messages directly from
a god and to have supernatural powers, such
as healing. Others are venerated as teachers
of exceptional insight; a New Religion may have
a founder of the first type who is succeeded
by a leader of the second type. Japanese New
Religions tend to focus on concerns in this world,
particularly health and personal success. The
most successful Japanese New Religion is Soka
Gakkai; this group emphasizes the traditional
Buddhist practice of chanting the sacred text
of the *Lotus Sutra*, but it teaches that this
will have concrete material as well as spiritual
benefits. Some New Religions also assimilate
ideas from Christianity or from popular culture.

RELATED RELIGIONS
See also
MAHAYANA BUDDHISM
Page 40
SHINTO
Page 54
TENRIKYO
Page 132

3-SECOND BIOGRAPHIES
NAKAYAMA MIKI
1798–1887

KAWATE BUNJIRO
1814–1883

DEGUCHI NAO
1836–1918

DAISAKU IKEDA
1928–

SHOKO ASAHARA
1955–

30-SECOND TEXT
Richard Bartholomew

*The New Religions of
Japan are grounded in
Buddhism and Shinto,
but reinterpreted for
a modern Japan by
influential leaders.*

3-SECOND SERMON
Religion in Japan is
renewed and made
relevant through the
revelations and insights
of founders and teachers.

3-MINUTE THEOLOGY
New Religions often face
suspicion or ridicule from
wider society, and media
reports on Japanese New
Religions have often
focused on particularly
eccentric groups with
leaders who, to outside
observers, appear to be
dishonest or deluded.
There has been less
tolerance for New
Religions in Japan since
the Tokyo terrorist attack
of 1995, when Aum
Shinrikyo unleashed poison
gas on the public as a
result of its beliefs about
the end of the world.

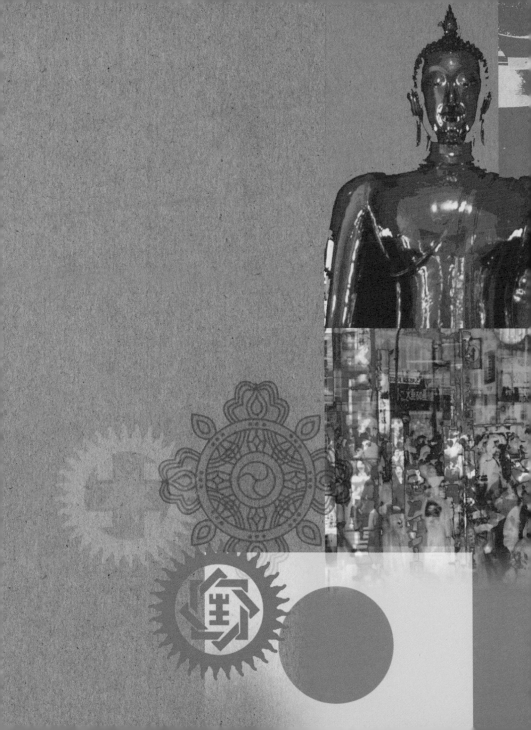

APPENDICES

RESOURCES

BOOKS

Animism: Respecting the Living World
Graham Harvey
(Columbia University Press, 2005)

A Brief Introduction to Hinduism
A. L. Herman
(Westview Press, 1991)

Buddhist Religions: A Historical Introduction
Richard H. Robinson, Willard L. Johnson, and Thanissaro Bhikkhu
(Wadsworth, 2004)

Christian Theology. An Introduction
Alister E. McGrath
(Wiley-Blackwell, 2010)

Contemporary Paganism: Listening People, Speaking Earth
Graham Harvey
(NYU Press, 2000)

Encountering Religion: An Introduction to the Religions of the World
Ian Markham and Tinu Ruparell (eds)
(Wiley-Blackwell, 2001)

Historical Dictionary of Shamanism
Graham Harvey and Robert J. Wallis
(The Scarecrow Press Inc., 2007)

Judaism
Nicholas de Lange
(Oxford University Press, 2003)

Magic and the Millennium: A Sociological Study of Religious Movements of Protest among Tribal and Third-World Peoples
Bryan R. Wilson
(Harper & Row, 1973)

The New Believers: A Survey of Sects, Cults and Alternative Religions
David V. Barrett
(Cassell, 2001)

A New Dictionary of Religions
John R. Hinnells (ed.)
(Wiley-Blackwell, 1995)

New Religions: A Guide—New Religious Movements, Sects and Alternative Spiritualities
Christopher Partridge and J. Gordon Melton
(Oxford University Press, 2004)

The Oxford Handbook of New Religious Movements
James R. Lewis
(Oxford University Press, 2008)

Religion in China
Richard C. Bush
(Argus, 1978)

Religion in Contemporary Japan
Ian Reader
(University of Hawaii Press, 1991)

Religions in Focus: New Approaches to Tradition and Contemporary Practices
Graham Harvey (ed.)
(Equinox Publishing, 2009)

Religions in the Modern World
Linda Woodhead, Hiroko Kawanami,
and Christopher Partridge (eds)
(Routledge, 2009)

*Western Muslims and the
Future of Islam*
Tariq Ramadan
(Oxford University Press, 2005)

A World Religions Reader
Ian Markham and Christy Lohr (eds)
(Wiley-Blackwell, 2009)

MAGAZINES/JOURNALS

*International Journal for the Study
of New Religions*
http://www.equinoxjournals.com/IJSNR

*The Journal of the American
Academy of Religion*
http://jaar.oxfordjournals.org/

Journal of Contemporary Religion
http://www.tandf.co.uk/journals/cjcr

The Journal of Religion
http://www.journals.uchicago.edu

The Journal of Religion and Society
http://moses.creighton.edu/JRS/

Reviews in Religion and Theology
http://www.blackwellpublishing.com/
journal.asp

WEB SITES

ABC Online Religion and Ethics Portal
http://www.abc.net.au/religion/
Collection of articles, commentaries, and
interviews on religious and ethical subjects
hosted by Australian broadcaster ABC.

BBC Religion
http://www.bbc.co.uk/religion/
Portal to articles and links about religions
and religious subjects, hosted by British
broadcaster BBC.

CESNUR: Center for Studies on New Religions
http://www.cesnur.org/
An international network of associations of
scholars working in the field of new religious
movements.

*INFORM: Information Network Focus on
Religious Movements*
http://www.inform.ac/
An independent charity providing balanced,
up-to-date information about new and
alternative religions or spiritual movements.

Religion Online
http://www.religion-online.org
Collection of scholarly articles, mainly from a
Christian perspective.

The Religion Hub
http://www.thereligionhub.com/
Interactive social network for people
interested in religion.

NOTES ON CONTRIBUTORS

Richard Bartholomew has a Ph.D. from the School of Oriental and African Studies, University of London, UK and he has published articles on the subject of religion and media. He runs a blog on religion and current affairs, which can be found here: http://barthsnotes.wordpress.com/. He also compiles indexes for academic books on religion.

Mathew Guest is senior lecturer in the department of Theology and Religion at Durham University, UK. He teaches classes in the study of religion, religion in contemporary Britain, and religious innovations in the modern world, and his research focuses on the sociology of contemporary evangelical Christianity. He is the author and editor of five books, including *Bishops, Wives and Children: Spiritual Capital Across the Generations* (with Douglas Davies), *Congregational Studies in the UK: Christianity in a Post-Christian Context* (edited with Karin Tusting and Linda Woodhead), *Religion and Knowledge: Sociological Perspectives* (edited with Elisabeth Arweck) and *Evangelical Identity and Contemporary Culture: A Congregational Study in Innovation*.

Graham Harvey is Reader in Religious Studies at The Open University, UK, where he cochairs the M.A. in Religious Studies. His research is mostly concerned with contemporary indigenous people, especially in North America and Oceania, but also in diaspora. He has also published about Paganism. Much of his teaching-related work engages with Judaism, pilgrimage, and the performance of religion.

Russell Re Manning is an Affiliated Lecturer at the Faculty of Divinity and a Fellow of St. Edmund's College at the University of Cambridge, UK. His interests include philosophy of religion, theology and the arts, and the science-religion dialogue. His books include *The Oxford Handbook of Natural Theology* and *The Cambridge Companion to Paul Tillich*.

Alexander Studholme is Lecturer in Indian Religions at the School of Theology and Religious Studies at Bangor University in Wales. His interests include mantras, Jungian approaches to Buddhism, and the Wisdom Christianity of Bede Griffiths. He is a member of the Dzogchen Community of the Tibetan lama, Namkhai Norbu Rinpoche. He is the author of *The Origins of Om Manipadme Hum, A Study of the Karandavyuha Sutra*.

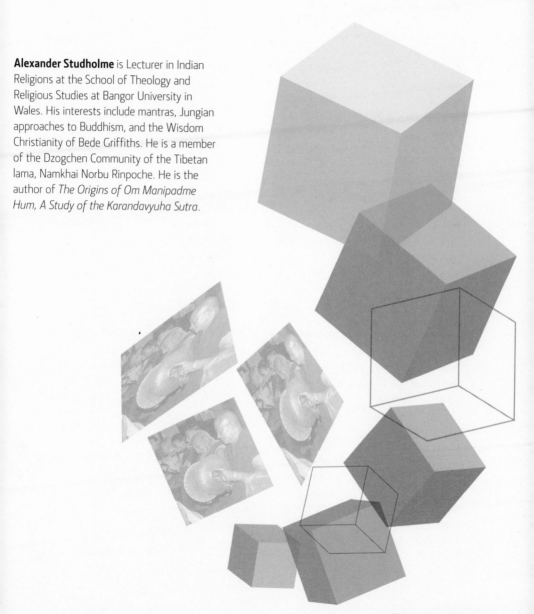

INDEX

ACKNOWLEDGMENTS

PICTURE CREDITS
The publisher would like to thank the following
individuals and organizations for their kind
permission to reproduce the images in this book.
Every effort has been made to acknowledge the
pictures, however we apologize if there are any
unintentional omissions.

Alamy/Biju: 34; Imagebroker: 38; Doug Steley C.: 52.
Corbis/Reuters/Munish Sharma: 46.
iStockphoto/Karim Hesham: 70.